I0776081

# A Condensed Anti-Slavery Bible Argument

# By a Citizen of Virginia

## George Bourne

# A
# CONDENSED ANTI-SLAVERY
# BIBLE ARGUMENT;
# BY A CITIZEN OF VIRGINIA.

"Woo to them that call evil good, and good evil," &c.--*Isa.* v. 20.
"To the law and to the testimony," &c.--*Isa.* vii. 20.
"Prove all things; hold fast that which is good."--*Thess.* v. 21.

## LARGE PRINT EDITION

NEW YORK:
PRINTED BY S. W. BENEDICT,
NO. 16 SPRUCE STREET.
1845.

# CONTENTS.


- INTRODUCTION..... 10
- CHAPTER I.
  DEFINITIONS.....14
- CHAPTER II.
  MAN-STEALING.....18
- CHAPTER III.
  PERVERSIONS OF THE SCRIPTURES....
- CHAPTER IV.
  CASE OF CAIN.....
- CHAPTER V.
  CASE OF CANAAN.....
- CHAPTER VI.
  RULES OF CONSTRUCTION.....
- CHAPTER VII.
  USES OF THE WORDS "BUY" AND "SELL." ...
- CHAPTER VIII.
  THE TRUE ISSUE.....
- CHAPTER X.
  KEY TO THE INQUIRY.....
- CHAPTER X.
  PRO-SLAVERY PERVERSIONS OF THE OLD TESTAMENT.....
  Examination of Gen. xii. 5, xvii. 12, 13, 23, 27; xx. 14; xxiv. 35.

- CHAPTER XI.
  PRO-SLAVERY PERVERSIONS OF THE OLD TESTAMENT. . . . .
  Examination of Ex. xii. 43, 45, xx. 17, xxi 2-6, 7, 11, 20, 21; Deut. xv. 12-18, xxi. 10, 14.
- CHAPTER XII.
  PRO-SLAVERY PERVERSIONS OF THE OLD TESTAMENT. . . . .
  Examination of Lev. xxv. 39-43, 44-46, 47-54.
- CHAPTER XIII.
  PRO-SLAVERY PERVERSIONS OF THE OLD TESTAMENT. . . . .
  Examination of Deut. xx. 10-20; Josh. ix. 22, 23, 27; 1 Kings ix. 21, 26; 2 Kings iv. 1, &c. Neh. v. 5-13; Jer. xxxiv. 8-17.
- CHAPTER XIV.
  TWELVE CIRCUMSTANTIAL FACTS. . . .
- CHAPTER XV.
  PRO-SLAVERY PERVERSIONS OF THE NEW TESTAMENT. . . . .
- CHAPTER XVI.
  PRO-SLAVERY PERVERSIONS OF THE NEW TESTAMENT. . . . .
  Examination of Matt. xx. 28, xxvi. 28; Acts xx. 28; Rom. vii. 14; 1 Cor. vi. 20, vii. 23; 1 Pet. i. 18, 19; 2 Pet ii. 1, 3; Rev. v. 9, &c.

- CHAPTER XVII.
  PRO-SLAVERY PERVERSIONS OF THE
  NEW TESTAMENT......
  Examination of Matt xviii. 23, 25, xxii. 27;
  Rom. xiii. 1-7; Titus iii. 1; 1 Pet. ii. 13.
- CHAPTER XVIII.
  PRO-SLAVERY PERVERSIONS OF THE
  NEW TESTAMENT......
  Examination of Eph. vi. 5-9; Col. iii. 22-25,
  iv. 1; Titus ii 9, 10; 1 Tim. vi. 1; 1 Pet. ii. 18-
  20.
- CHAPTER XIX.
  PRO-SLAVERY PERVERSIONS OF THE
  NEW TESTAMENT......
  Examination of the Epistle to Philemon.
- CHAPTER XX.
  CONCLUSION--REFLECTIONS......

# A CONDENSED ANTI-SLAVERY BIBLE ARGUMENT.

# INTRODUCTION.

THE belief was long nearly universal, and is yet very general throughout the Christian world, that the Scriptures do, to some extent, justify human slavery, as practiced in this country. The object of the following chapters is to controvert this belief, and to prove that it is false and heretical, as well as dangerous and destructive to human happiness; that this belief is founded entirely on perversions of the true meaning of certain passages in the Scriptures, and is entirely contrary to the spirit of the divine volume, the letter of which condemns the practice with as much severity as it did that of any other crime. The following *argument* is presented for the calm and prayerful consideration of all Christians, both in the *North* and in the *South*. The time has come when (as a learned writer justly remarks[*]),

*"neither the evidences of the Gospel, nor the solemnities of religion; neither the constitution of the church, nor the rights of its members; neither the divine right of bishops, nor the value of holy orders; neither the spirituality of the soul, nor the materiality of the body, can escape the ordeal*

*of free and full discussion. Shall we, then, think it strange that American slavery, with all its influences on the moral and political destinies of this great and mighty nation, shall, by the spontaneous concession of the whole civilized world, be allowed to escape inquiry, or be exempt from appearing in the presence of this august and powerful tribunal of FREE DISCUSSION? It cannot be imagined. Come it must, and come it will; and we may as well be prepared for it soon as late."*

*Millennial Harbinger, vol. ii., ¶3, p. 50.

Do not, kind reader, throw this aside, as the production of an *Abolitionist*, but read it as the candid convictions of "A CITIZEN OF VIRGINIA," who has thought much on the subject, and examined critically the Bible with reference to his duty and obligations to those unfortunate beings who are held in bondage. My treating of the difficult, and to many, offensive subject of slavery, does not arise from any want of attachment to the South, or any disregard to its interests, much less does it arise from a disposition to trifle with the wishes or fears of those who may have fears on this matter. If I believed that discussion would have the effect that some apprehend from it, it would be with me a weighty consideration against ever publishing one line on the subject. But after looking at the matter on all sides, and giving it a good deal of consideration, I am strongly inclined to the opinion that the danger attending slavery in the South depends very little, if at all, on a temperate discussion of the subject.

A multitude of things must ever bind my affections to the South. I was born on the banks of Virginia's beautiful river Potomac, where my parents spent a considerable portion of their existence, almost in sight of the place where the mortal remains of Washington are deposited. Almost all my relations are there, or in slaveholding states. All my early associations, all those untold bonds that bind us to the scenes of infancy and youth, most of those moral ties which unite us to those we love, for whom we have often prayed, and with whom we have taken "sweet counsel together, and walked unto the house of God in company"--are Virginians.

"With all thy faults I love thee still, my country--and still must love thee."

Fellow-citizens, examine with me this important subject--and follow the guidance of the "lamp of life" in the path of *duty,* which is the sure road to Heaven. And let us remember "the example of Virginia's noblest son, the Father of his country, who at the last hour, when the soul, in the light of an approaching eternity, sees with peculiar clearness the boundaries which separate the wrong from the right, *restored his slaves to their natural rights.*" And let us imitate one of Kentucky's bright stars, C. M. Clay, who in the face of all opposition emancipated THIRTEEN slaves, while yet in health of mind and body.

# CHAPTER I.

## DEFINITIONS.

IN order the better to understand the subject it is necessary here to introduce a few plain definitions. Slavery has two definitions--the direct and the indirect. The first of these is that it is the total deprivation of human rights; the other that it is the reducing of human beings to the condition of property, the same as other goods, wares, merchandise and chattels. Either of these definitions will answer for the purpose of argument, though the latter is to be preferred, because it is the most familiar. There are a variety of other ways in which mankind hold control over each other, and sometimes unjustly and oppressively; but if the persons controlled be not held as property, they are not slaves. A Right is defined to be, the privilege or liberty of being, doing, having or suffering something at our own pleasure and discretion without the interference, interruption or hindrance of others--and to this discretion neither the law of God, nor the common law, nor any other just law, sets any other bounds than that we so exercise our own rights as not to infringe the same rights in other human beings. A

Wrong is defined to be, any voluntary act which disturbs, interrupts, hinders, or destroys the free exercise of the rights of others--every such act being strictly forbidden by the law of God, and every other just law. Right and Wrong are, therefore, the everlasting moral and political opposites and antagonists of each other. Mr. Weld, in his valuable "Bible Argument," says, "ENSLAVING MEN IS REDUCING THEM TO ARTICLES OF PROPERTY -- making free agents, chattels--converting *persons* into *things*--sinking immortality into *merchandize. A slave* is one held in this condition. In law, he owns nothing and can acquire nothing." His right to himself is abrogated. If he says *my* hands, *my* body, *my* mind, MY*self,* they are figures of speech. To *use himself* for his own good is a *crime.* To keep what he *earns* is stealing. To take his body into his own keeping is insurrection. In a word, the profit of his master is made the END of his being, and he a *mere means* to that end--a mere means to an end into which his interests do not enter-- of which they constitute no portion. MAN sunk to a thing! The intrinsic element, the *principle* of slavery. MEN, bartered, leased, mortgaged, bequeathed, invoiced, shipped in cargoes, stored as goods, taken on executions, and knocked off at public outcry! Their *rights,* another's conveniences; their interests, wares on sale; their happiness, a household utensil; their personal inalienable ownership, a serviceable article or a plaything, as best suits the humor of the hour; their deathless nature, conscience, social affections, sympathies, hopes--marketable commodities! We repeat it, "THE REDUCTION OF PERSONS TO THINGS!" Not robbing a man of privileges, but of *himself*; not loading him with burdens, but making him *a beast of burden*; not restraining liberty, but subverting it; not curtailing rights, but abolishing them; not inflicting personal cruelty, but annihilating *personality*; not exacting involuntary labor, but sinking man into an *implement* of labor; not abridging human comforts, but abrogating *human nature*; not depriving an animal of immunities, but despoiling a rational being of attributes, uncreating A MAN to make room for *a thing*! That this is American slavery is shown by the laws of the slave states. Judge Stroud, in his "Sketch of the Laws relating to Slavery," says, "The cardinal principle of slavery, that the slave is not to be ranked among sentient beings but among *things*, obtains as undoubted law in all of these (the slave) states." The law of South Carolina says,--[*]

*Brev. Dig., 229.

"Slaves shall be deemed, held, taken, reputed and adjudged in law to be chattels personal in the hands of their owners and possessors, and their executors, administrators, and assigns, TO ALL INTENTS, CONSTRUCTIONS, AND PURPOSES WHATSOEVER."

In Louisiana, "A slave is one who is in the power of a master, to whom he belongs; the master may sell him, dispose of his person, his industry and his labor; he can do nothing, possess nothing, nor acquire anything but what belongs to his master. Civ. Code, Art. 35." Tried by these definitions, human slavery is one of the greatest wrongs existing in the world.

# CHAPTER II.

## MAN-STEALING.

THE practice of human slavery is not condemned in the Scriptures by that name, nor mentioned in any of our common law definitions by the same name. But it is condemned in the Scriptures under other names, and by descriptions, plainly and severely. There are many modern practices, such as piracy, dueling, gambling, &c., which are not condemned in the Scriptures by those names, but by descriptions. In this way, though all the crimes against God and his religion have been legalized by men in this world, they are all plainly described and condemned in the Scriptures, so that mankind are without any moral or just excuse for committing them. But that the practice of human slavery is thus condemned, is plainly proven, as follows:--

I. By our slaveholding definitions, human slavery is described as property in man, and slaves are declared to be the property of their masters or owners, and cannot own, possess, or enjoy anything but what belongs to their owners. But by our common law definitions, human slavery is compounded of the crimes of kidnapping, assault and battery, and false imprisonment.

In [1] Ex. xxi. 16 is a short description of the kidnapping and sale of one person by another, described as "man-stealing," the same being an entirely different transaction from the voluntary sales of servants by themselves, as described in [2] Gen. xlvii. 19-23,

1 And he that stealeth a man, and selleth him, or if he be found in his hand, he shall surely be put to death.--Ex. xxi. 16.

2 Wherefore shall we die before thine eyes, both we and our land? buy us and our land for bread, and we and our land will be servants unto Pharaoh: and give us seed, that we may live, and not die, that the land be not desolate. And Joseph bought all the land of Egypt for Pharaoh; for the Egyptians sold every man his field, because the famine prevailed over them: so the land became Pharaoh's. And as for the people, he removed them to cities from one end of the borders of Egypt even to the other end thereof. Only the land of the priests bought he not; for the priests had a portion *assigned them* of Pharaoh, and did eat their portion which Pharaoh gave them; wherefore they sold not their lands. Then Joseph said unto the people, Behold, I have bought you this day and your land for Pharaoh: lo, here is seed for you, and ye shall sow the land.-- Gen. xlvii. 19-23.

## [3]Ex. xxi. 2-6,

3 If thou buy a Hebrew servant, six years he shall serve: and in the seventh he shall go out free for nothing. If he came in by

himself, he shall go out by himself: if he were married, then his wife shall go out with him. If his master have given him a wife and she have borne him sons or daughters, the wife and her children shall be her master's, and he shall go out by himself. And if the servant shall plainly say, I love my master, my wife, and my children; I will not go out free: then his master shall bring him unto the judges: he shall also bring him to the door, or unto the door-post: and his master shall bore his ear through with an awl; and he shall serve him forever.-- Ex. xxi. 2-6.

# [4]Lev. xxv. 39-47,

4 And if thy brother that dwelleth by thee be waxen poor, and be sold unto thee; thou shalt not compel him to serve as a bond-servant. But as a hired servant, and as a sojourner he shall be with thee, and shall serve thee unto the year of jubilee: And then shall he depart from thee, both he and his children with him, and shall return unto his own family, and unto the possession of his fathers shall he return. For they are my servants, which I brought forth out of the land of Egypt; they shall not be sold as bond-men. Thou shalt not rule over him with rigor, but shalt fear thy God. Both thy bond-men, and thy bond-maids, which thou shalt have, shall be of the heathen that are round about you; of them shall ye buy bond-men and bond-maids. Moreover, of the children of the strangers that do sojourn among you, of them shall ye buy, and of their families that are with you, which they begat in your land: and they shall be your possession. And ye shall take them as an inheritance for your children after you, to inherit them for a possession, they shall be your bond-men for ever: but over your brethren the children of Israel, ye shall not rule one over another with rigor. And if a sojourner or a stranger wax rich by thee, and thy brother that dwelleth by him wax poor, and sell himself unto the stranger or sojourner by thee, or to the stock of the stranger's family:--Lev. xxv. 39-47.

[5]Deut. xv. 12, &c.

5 And if thy brother, a Hebrew man, or a Hebrew woman, be sold unto thee, and serve thee six years; then in the seventh year thou shalt let him go free from thee--Deut. xv. 12.

By force of this one short Levitical statute, the act of *man-stealing* (kidnapping), *man-selling* (slave-trading), and *man-holding* (slaveholding), are, like several other crimes, condemned by the Levitical law; declared by the statute to be punishable with *sure death*--it being very remarkable that the sentence of punishment is expressed in the strongest terms, see [1]Lev. xxiv. 17, thereby indicating that, in the sight of God, these acts are equal to the greatest crimes in guilt and enormity. The statute is also highly descriptive of property in man, or slavery; for one adult person seldom ever seizes and sells another, or holds him in subjection to himself, except as an article of property, or as a slave.

1 And he that killeth any man shall surely be put to death.-- Lev. xxiv. 17.

[2]Numb. xxxv. 30, 31, &c.

2 Whoso killeth any person, the murderer shall be put to death by the mouth of witnesses: but one witness shall not testify against any person to cause him to die. Moreover, ye shall take no satisfaction for the life of a murderer, which is guilty of death: but he shall surely be put to death.--Numb. Div. 30, 31.

II. But if there could be a reasonable doubt of the intent to describe a property or slavish title, by the acts condemned in the foregoing statute, it is entirely dispelled by the description of the same crime in [3]Deut. xxiv. 7;

3 If a man be found stealing any of his brethren of the children of Israel, and maketh merchandise of him, or selleth him; then that thief shall die; and thou shalt put evil away from among you.--Deut. xxiv. 7.

where, in addition to the other description, the crime is still further described as the "making merchandise of," the person stolen, as men seldom "make merchandise of," or trade, or traffic in anything which they do not regard and treat as property. It is true, that the same phrase has a different meaning in [1]2 Peter ii. 3,

1 And through covetousness shall they with feigned words make merchandise of you: whose judgment now of a long time lingereth not, and their damnation slumbereth not.--2 Pet. ii. 3.

but what puts our interpretation of the principal text beyond a doubt, is the fact that the criminal is described as a "thief," for real thieves never steal anything but what they consider property, and which they hold, "make merchandise of," and otherwise treat as property. We know by the description of "feigned words," or false and deceitful religious instruction, used in 2 Peter ii. 3, that the foregoing phrase is there used to describe ecclesiastical oppression, such as is condemned in [2]Matt. xxiii. 4-14,

2 For they bind heavy burdens, and grievous to be borne, and lay them on men's shoulders; but they themselves will not move them with one of their fingers. But all their works they do for to be seen of men: they make broad their phylacteries, and enlarge the borders of their garments, and love the uppermost rooms at feasts, and the chief seats in the synagogues, and greetings in the markets, and to be called of men, Rabbi, Rabbi. But be not ye called Rabbi: for one is your Master, even Christ; and all ye are brethren. And call no man your father upon the earth; for one is your Father which is in heaven. Neither be ye called masters: for one is Your Master, even Christ. But he that is greatest among you, shall be your servant. And whosoever shall exalt himself, shall be abased; and he that shall humble himself shall be exalted. But woe unto you, scribes and Pharisees, hypocrites! for ye shut up the kingdom of heaven against men: for ye neither go in yourselves, neither suffer ye them that are entering to go in. Woo unto you, scribes and Pharisees, hypocrites! for ye devour widows' houses, and for a pretence make long prayer: therefore ye shall receive the greater damnation.--Matt. xxiii. 4-14.

and other passages, and has been practiced in every age of the Christian church, and by nothing, perhaps, in so high and destructive a degree, as by the false instruction, that human slavery is morally justified by the Scriptures.

III. The subject is perfectly illustrated in the seizure and sale of Joseph by his brethren to the Ishmaelite's, and by the latter to Potiphar, [3]Gen. xxxvii. 23, 28, 36.

3 And it came to pass when Joseph was come unto his brethren, that they stripped Joseph out of his coat, his coat of many colors that was on him. And they took him and cast him into a pit: and the pit was empty, there was no water in it. And they sat down to eat bread: and they lifted up their eyes and looked, and behold a company of Ishmaelite's came from Gilead, with their camels bearing spicery, and balm, and myrrh, going to carry it down to Egypt. And Judah said unto his brethren, What profit is it if we slay our brother, and conceal his blood! Come, and let us sell him to the Ishmaelite's, and let not our hand be upon him; for he is our brother and our flesh: and his brethren were content. Then there passed by Midianites, merchantmen; and they drew up Joseph out of the pit, and sold Joseph to the Ishmaelite's for twenty pieces of silver: and they brought Joseph into Egypt. And the Midianites sold him into Egypt unto Potiphar, an officer of Pharaoh's, and captain of the guard.-- Gen. xxxvii. 23-28, 36.

Here is a case described at length, of the forcible seizure or kidnapping of one person by others, of his sale as an article of merchandise or property by them to others still for money, and of the subsequent sale of him as property by the purchasers to another, all exactly as our slave seizures, and sales, and purchases are now made. This transaction is represented in Gen. xlii. 21, 22,[1]

*1 And they said one to another, We are verily guilty concerning our brother, in that we saw the anguish of his soul, when he besought us, and we would not hear; therefore is this distress come upon us. And Reuben answered them, saying, Spake I not unto you saying, Do not sin against the child; and ye would not hear; therefore behold also his blood is required.--Gen. xlii. 21, 22.*

as worthy of the punishment of death in those guilty of it, as a self-evident and enormous crime against the law of Nature. In Joseph's own description of the transaction he states that he was "*stolen,*" [2]Gen. xl. 15.

2 For indeed I was stolen away out of the land of the Hebrews: and here also have I done nothing that they should put me into the dungeon.--Gen. xl. 15.

The crime committed upon him was, therefore, stealing, and as he was a man that crime was "man stealing," the nature and consequences of which were precisely the same as those which everywhere uniformly attend the practice of human slavery, or in other words, they are each precisely the same crime. It should be remarked in further illustration, that the barbarities and horrors which uniformly attend the practice of human slavery, as incidents to it, absolutely necessary to its support, are not recorded in this case as a part of the great crime so severely condemned. Notwithstanding his "anguish of soul," Gen. xlii. 21, we do not know but Joseph was as "well treated" as the best conditioned of our slaves now are. The whole moral guilt of the transaction is represented in the passage quoted, as consisting in the conversion of Joseph into an article of property, or rendering him a slave. This case is also highly instructive by its teaching us that human slavery is as great a crime against the law of nature, as it is against the Scriptures or law of Revelation. The latter not having been revealed to the Patriarchs, they were left to the guidance furnished by the dim light of the former, in consequence of which they committed many crimes, against both of these laws, of which they did not become sensible till they were brought into deep trouble by the same.

By similar means the strongest advocates of human slavery may be convinced of its deep natural as well as revealed criminality, and it is indeed often the last argument that can be effectually used with such persons. Let them and their relations and friends be but once enslaved themselves, and they will as readily see and acknowledge the natural and moral guilt of the practice, as Joseph's brethren did.

IV. The same doctrine is also evident from the literal meaning of the Greek word *andrapodistai*, translated "men-stealers," [3] 1 Tim. i. 10,

3 For whoremongers, for them that defile themselves with mankind, for men-stealers, for liars, for perjured persons, and if there be any other thing that is contrary to sound doctrine.--1 Tim. 1. 10.

as well as from the class of crimes connected with it in that and the preceding verse, for according to this connection, whatever man-stealing be, it is equal to murder and the greatest and worst of other crimes in enormity, and just as deserving of death by the Levitical or moral law. But this word (*andrapodistai*) literally means "slave-owners" or "slaveholders," as Greek readers well know, and ought to have been rendered "slaveholders" to have a literal English translation. The ancient Greek and Roman "*andrapodistai*" were *bonâ fide* slaveholders "to all intents, constructions and purposes," holding exactly the same relation to their slaves that our American slaveholders do to theirs, as ancient Greek and Roman history fully testifies. But I do not complain of any perversion in the common English translation, for I have not the least doubt but what the men-stealers, men-sellers, men-buyers and men-holders described in [1]Ex. xxi. 16, and [2]Deut. xxiv. 7, were *bonâ fide* slaveholders, so that since man-stealing, &c., and human slavery are the same identical crime, either translation is correct; nor do I care which translation our modern advocates of slavery prefer, for according to the literal spirit and meaning of the principal text and its connection, the practice of slavery is as great a crime as murder, &c., and equally deserving the punishment of death as they are. The Greek word for slave is *andrapoda* (literally *man foot*, or, man-trodden under foot), while the word for "slaveholders" is *andrapodistai* (literally *men feet owners or holders*), exactly corresponding in meaning with our English words "slaves" and "slaveholders;" just as the practice of ancient Grecian slavery exactly corresponded, in every material respect, with that pursued in the

United States. As human slavery is a practice entirely of heathen origin, it was to be expected that when it was adopted among Christians from the heathen, it would in a material respect be supported by the same means, appear the same thing both in practice and name, and so far as its influence extended heathenize those Christians that adopted it.

*1 And he that stealeth a man, and selleth him, or if he be found in his hand he shall surely be put to death.--Ex. xxi. 16.*

*2 If a man be found stealing any of his brethren of the children of Israel, and maketh merchandise of him, or selleth him; then that thief shall die; and thou shalt put evil away from among you.--Deut. xxiv. 7.*

V. The same doctrine is strongly corroborated by the language used in James v. 4, and its connection or context. "Behold the hire of the laborers which have reaped down your fields which is of you kept back by fraud, crieth; and the cries of them which have reaped, are entered into the ears of the Lord of Sabbath." Language like this imports death and destruction all over the Scriptures, as punishments due to the greatest crimes only. In the wide Roman Empire, where most of the Apostles resided and preached, there were no other laborers except slaves but what were entitled to and received wages by law, so that the Apostle in this passage must have referred to slaves and to their condition and treatment alone, as evidence of the greatest criminality in their owners. And since the Apostle's language imports in the Scripture sense death and destruction as punishment due to the greatest crimes only, we necessarily infer from such premises, as a plain Bible doctrine, that human slavery is a crime justly deserving the punishment of death in those who practice it. No opposite inference can be justly derived from the passage.

VI. The same doctrine is also evident from the description of one of the crimes of the mystical "Mother of Harlots" in [1]Rev. xviii. 13, which was "merchandise (that is trading in as property) * * * and *slaves* and souls of men," which so far as it goes is an exact description of human slavery. As death and destruction are represented in this chapter as punishments justly due to those who pursue this kind of merchandise or traffic, we are also compelled to draw the same inference as the foregoing. This inference is strongly corroborated by the fact, that most of the objects enumerated in the passage are morally lawful subjects of trade and traffic, and as these terrible punishments were justly due for crime of some kind, they must at any rate have been for that of trading in slaves--a terrible warning to us not to pursue the practice of any mixture of good and evil. The mystical character here described is generally believed among Protestants to mean the Roman Catholic Church, and as a historical fact worthy of notice in this connection it is proper to state, that the practice of negro slavery among Christians, as well as the scriptural perversions by which it was justified, first originated among the members of that Church, though as the same wicked practice and perversions were immediately adopted by the various Protestant sects, the inference has been drawn that they are the *daughters* of "the Mother of Harlots," [2]Rev. xvii. 5, and will partake of the punishment for her sins, so far as they have been guilty of her crimes.

*1 And cinnamon, and odors, and ointments, and frankincense, and wine, and oil, and fine flour, and wheat, and beasts, and sheep, and horses, and chariots, and slaves, and souls of men.--Rev. xviii. 13.*

*2 And upon her forehead was a name written, MYSTERY, BABYLON THE GREAT, THE MOTHER OF HARLOTS AND ABOMINATIONS OF THE EARTH.-- Rev. xviii. 5.*

VII. The same doctrine is also strongly to be inferred from the natural import of the language used in such passages as [1]Jer. xxii. 13, [2]Hab. ii. 9-11; [3]Mal. iii. 5, &c. where the compulsory labor of the poor and helpless without wages, as in the case of slaves, is threatened with the temporal if not the eternal destruction of those who practice this kind of oppression, such destruction as the scriptural use of the word "*woe*" always imports. Certainly these terrible passages include the case of oppressed slaves and their oppressive owners, if they do or can any case. So the depriving the poor and helpless of the wages justly due them for labor and other services performed, is everywhere denounced in the Scriptures as one of the greatest sins that men can commit, and as sure to be punished with the utter destruction of the criminals and their families and posterity, see [4]Ex. xxii. 22-24; [9]Prov. xxii. 22, 23, &c. as these passages certainly include the case of slaves and their enslavers, so their moral teaching is, that God will punish with utter retributive destruction those who practice the sin of slavish oppression.

*1 Woo unto him that buildeth his house by unrighteousness, and his chambers by wrong; that useth his neighbor's service without wages, and giveth him not for his work.-- Jer. xxii. 13.*

*2 Woo to him that coveteth an evil covetousness to his house, that he may set his nest on high, that he may be delivered from the power of evil! Thou hast consulted shame to thy house by cutting off many people, and hast sinned against thy soul. For the stone shall cry out of the wall, and the beam out of the timber shall answer it.--Hab. ii. 9-11.*

*3 And I will come near to you to judgment, and I will be a swift witness against the sorcerers, and against the adulterers, and against false swearers, and against those that oppress the hireling in his wages, the widow, and the fatherless, and that turn aside the stranger from his right, and fear not me, saith the LORD of hosts.--Mal. iii. 5.*

*4 Ye shall not afflict any widow, or fatherless child. If thou afflict them in any wise, and they cry at all unto me, I will surely hear their cry; and my wrath shall wax hot, and I will kill you with the sword; and your wives shall be widows, and your children fatherless.--Ex. xxii. 22-24*

*[5]Lev. xix. 13;*

*5 Thou shalt not defraud thy neighbor, neither rob him: the wages of him that is hired shall not abide with thee all night until the morning.--Lev. xix. 13.*

*[6]Deut. xv. 9;*

*6 Beware that there be not a thought in thy wicked heart, saying, The seventh year, the year of release, is at hand; and thine eye be evil against thy poor brother, and thou givest him naught; and he cry unto the LORD against thee, and it be sin unto thee.--Deut. xv. 9.*

*Deut. [7]xxiv. 14, 15;*

*7 Thou shalt not oppress a hired servant that is poor and needy, whether he be of thy brethren, or of thy strangers that are in thy land within thy gates: at his day thou shalt give him his hire, neither shall the sun go down upon it, for he is poor, and setteth his heart upon it: lest he cry against thee unto the LORD, and it be sin unto thee.-- Deut. xxiv. 14, 15.*

*[8]Job xxvii. 13-23;*

*8 This is the portion of a wicked man with God, and the heritage of oppressors, which they shall receive of the Almighty. If his children be multiplied, it is for the sword: and his offspring shall not be satisfied with bread. Those that remain of him shall be buried in death: and his widows shall not weep. Though he heap up silver as the dust, and prepare raiment as the clay; he may prepare it, but the just shall put it on, and the innocent shall divide the silver. He buildeth his house as a moth, and as a booth that the keeper maketh. The rich man shall lie down, but he shall not be gathered: he openeth his eyes, and he is not. Terrors take hold on him as waters, a tempest stealeth him away in the night. The east wind carrieth him away, and he departeth: and as a storm hurleth him out of his place. For God shall cast upon him, and not spare: he would fain flee out of his hand. Men shall clap their hands at him, and shall hiss him out of his place.--Job xxvii. 13-23.*

*9 Rob not the poor, because he is poor: neither oppress the afflicted in the gate: for the LORD will plead their cause, and spoil the soul of those that spoiled them.--Prov. xxii. 22,23.*

A Virginia preacher of the Gospel[*]
has said, "The fact that slavery was introduced
among us, not by ourselves, but by our forefathers,
is almost constantly brought forward as an excuse
for our practice. Admitting that this may be some
palliation, a moment's reflection might satisfy any
one that we are not justified in living in a practice
in itself wrong by the fact that our fathers acted so
before us. The laws of civil society, the conduct of
man with man, the history of God's dealings
towards nations and individuals, as well as the
express declarations of his Word, are all opposed to
this plea of justification. How can you read your
Bible and not see as a matter of fact, that the sins of
our fathers instead of justifying us in living in the
same, will assuredly, unless we repent, be visited
on us? It is laid down as a principle of God's
providential government that he will visit the sins
of the fathers on the children unto the third and
fourth generation. This is explained in Ezek. xviii.
as especially applicable to those cases in which
children continue in the same sins in which their
fathers lived. The way, and the only way, to escape
visitations for the sins of our fathers, is to forsake
those sins, and as far as may be correct the evils
they have done. Not only is this principle plainly

taught in Scripture, but it is illustrated by examples, and some on the very point in question.

** Rev. J. D. Paxton, formerly Pastor of the Cumberland Congregation , Virginia, in a book of 200 pages, entitled "Letters on Slavery," published by A. T. Skillman, Lexington., Ky., 1833.*

"The generation of the Egyptians that were visited with such heavy judgments for enslaving Israel, did not *begin* the work of enslaving that people; it was commenced long before. They found it in existence, received it from their fathers, and were probably the third or fourth generation that had practiced it. They followed the footsteps of their fathers; and while probably making this identical excuse, the cloud of vengeance was gathering over them, which swept over them as with the besom of destruction.

"So it was with the Babylonians, and the nations that acted with them, in oppressing Israel, that 'held them fast and refused to let them go.' God visited on them their own sins, and the sins of their fathers; gave them up to spoil and slavery, and caused it to 'be recompensed unto them according to their doings.' The practice of slavery may have been going on about as long among us as it did in

Egypt; and while some are pleading in excuse that we did not begin it, they seem to forget that, according to God's word, we are the generation at which the Divine threatening begins to look hard. The very fact that it has gone on so long, is in proof that the cup of iniquity must be filling up, and the bitter waters almost ready to overflow."

VIII. Abundant additional evidence of the same doctrine is found in the fact, that the holding, exchanging, bartering, buying, selling and otherwise trading, in human beings as property, and the licentiousness and prodigality, tyranny and cruelty produced by those practices are represented as among the greatest sins and threatened with the severest Divine judgments and punishments, in various other parts of the Scriptures, see [1]Deut. xxviii. 68;

*1 And the LORD shall bring thee into Egypt again with ships, by the way whereof I spoke unto thee, Thou shalt see it no more again: and there ye shall be sold unto your enemies for bond-men and bond-women, and no man shall buy you.--Deut. xxviii. 68.*

[2] *2 Chron. xxviii. 8-13;*

*2 And the children of Israel carried away captive of their brethren two hundred thousand, women, sons, and daughters, and took also away much spoil from them, and brought the spoil to Samaria. But a prophet of the LORD was there, whose name was Oded; and he went out before the host that came to Samaria, and said unto them, Behold, because the LORD God of your fathers was wroth with Judah, he hath delivered them into your hand, and ye have slain them in a rage that reacheth up to heaven. And now ye purpose to keep under the children of Judah and Jerusalem for bond-men and bond-women unto you: but are there not with you, even with you, sins against the LORD your God? Now hear me therefore, and deliver the captives again, which ye have taken captive of your brethren; for the fierce wrath of the LORD is upon you. Then certain of the heads of the children of Ephraim, Azariah the son of Johanan, Berechiah the son of Meshillemoth, and Jehizkiah the son of Shallum, and Amasa the son of Hadlai, stood up against them that came from the war, and said unto them, Ye shall not bring in the captives hither: for whereas we have offended against the Lord already, ye intend to add more to our sins and to our trespass: for our trespass is great, and there is fierce wrath against Israel. So the armed men left the captives and the spoil before the princes and all the congregation. And the men which were expressed by name rose up, and took the captives, and with the spoil clothed all that were naked among them, and arrayed them, and shod them, and gave them to eat and to drink, and anointed them, and carried all the feeble of them upon asses, and brought them to Jericho, the city of palm-trees, and to their brethren: then they returned to Samaria.--2 Chron. xxviii. 8-15.*

[3]Neh. v. 5-15;

*3 Yet now our flesh is as the flesh of our brethren, our children as their children: and lo, we bring into bondage our sons and our daughters to be servants, and some of our daughters are brought into bondage already: neither is it in our power to redeem them; for other men have our lands and vineyards. And I was very angry when I heard their cry and these words. Then I consulted with myself, and I rebuked the nobles, and the rulers, and said unto them, Ye exact usury, every one of his brother. And I set a great assembly against them. And I said unto them, We, after our ability, have redeemed our brethren the Jews, which were sold unto the heathen; and will ye even sell your brethren? or shall they be sold unto us? Then held they their peace, and found nothing to answer. Also I said, It is not good that ye do: ought ye not to walk in the fear of our God because of the reproach of the heathen our enemies? I likewise, and my brethren, and my servants might exact of them money and corn: I pray you, let us leave off this usury. Restore, I pray you, to them, even this day, their lands, their vineyards, their oliveyards, and their houses, also the hundredth part of the money, and of the corn, the wine, and the oil, that ye exact of them. Then said they, We will restore them, and will require nothing of them; so will we do as thou sayest. Then I called the priests, and took an oath of them, that they should do according to this promise. Also I shook my lap, and said, So God shake out every man from his house, and from his labor, that performeth not this promise, even thus be he shaken out, and emptied. And all the congregation said, Amen, and praise the Lord. And the people did according to this promise.--Neh. v. 5-15.*

[4]Ps. xliv. 12;

*4 Thou sellest thy people for naught, and dost not increase thy wealth by their price.--Ps. xliv. 12.*

[5]Isa. lii. 3-6;

*5 For thus saith the Lord, Ye have sold yourselves for naught; and ye shall be redeemed without money. For thus saith the Lord God, My people went down aforetime into Egypt to sojourn there; and the Assyrian oppressed them without cause. Now therefore, what have I here, saith the Lord, that my people is taken away for naught? they that rule over them make them to howl, saith the Lord; and my name continually every day is blasphemed. Therefore my people shall know my name; therefore they shall know in that day that I am he that doth speak: behold, it is I.--lii. 3-6.*

[6]Jer. xv. 13, 14;

*6 Thy substance and thy treasures will I give to the spoil without price, and that for all thy sins, even in all thy borders. And I will make thee to pass with thine enemies into a land which thou knowest not: for a fire is kindled in mine anger, which shall burn upon you.--Jer. xv. 13, 14.*

# [7]Eze. xxvii. 2, 13, 26-36;

*7 Now, thou son of man, take up a lamentation for Tyrus. Javan, Tubal, and Meshech, they were thy merchants: they traded the persons of men and vessels of brass in thy market. Thy rowers have brought thee into great waters: the east wind hath broken thee in the midst of the seas. Thy riches, and thy fairs, thy merchandise, thy mariners, and thy pilots, thy caulkers, and the occupiers of thy merchandise, and all thy men of war, that are in thee, and in all thy company which is in the midst of thee, shall fall into the midst of the seas in the day of thy ruin. The suburbs shall shake at the sound of the cry of thy pilots. And all that handle the oar, the mariners, and all the pilots of the sea, shall come down from their ships, they shall stand upon the land; and shall cause their voice to be heard against thee, and shall cry bitterly, and shall cast up dust upon their heads, they shall wallow themselves in the ashes: and they shall make themselves utterly bald for thee, and gird them with sackcloth, and they shall weep for thee with bitterness of heart and bitter wailing. And in their wailing they shall take up a lamentation for thee, and lament over thee, saying, What city is like Tyrus, like the destroyed in the midst of the sea? When thy wares went forth out the seas, thou filledst many people; thou didst enrich the kings of the earth with the multitude of thy riches and of thy merchandise. In the time when thou shalt be broken by the seas in the depths of the waters, thy merchandise and all thy company in the midst of thee shall fail. All the inhabitants of the isles shall be astonished at thee, and their kings shall be sore afraid, they shall be troubled in their countenance. The merchants among the people shall hiss at thee; thou shalt be a terror, and never shalt be any more.--Eze. xxvii. 2, 13, 26-36.*

## [8]Joel Joel iii. 3-8;

*8 And they have cast lots for my people; and have given a boy for a harlot, and sold a girl for wine, that they might drink. Yea, and what have ye to do with me, O Tyre, and Zidon, and all the coasts of Palestine? will ye render me a recompense? and if ye recompense me, swiftly and speedily will I return your recompense upon your own head; Because ye have taken my silver and my gold, and have carried into your temples my goodly pleasant things. The children also of Judah and the children of Jerusalem have ye sold unto the Grecians, that ye might remove them far from their border. Behold I will raise them out of the place whither ye have sold them, and will return your recompense upon your own head: and I will sell your sons and your daughters into the hand of the children of Judah, and they shall sell them to the Sabeans, to a people far off: for the Lord hath spoken it.--Joel iii. 3-8.*

## [9]Amos ii. 6, 7;

*9 Thus saith the Lord; For three transgressions of Israel, and for four, I will not turn away the punishment thereof: because they sold the righteous for silver, and the poor for a pair of shoes; that pant after the dust of the earth on the head of the poor, and turn aside the way of the meek; and a man and his father will go in unto the same maid, to profane my holy name.--Amos ii. 6, 7.*

[10]Oba. 11;

*10 In the day that thou stoodest on the other side, in the day that the strangers carried away captive his forces, and foreigners entered into his gates, and cast lots upon Jerusalem, even thou wast as one of them.--Oba. II.*

[11]Nah. iii. 10;

*11 Yet she was carried away, she went into captivity: her young children also were dashed in pieces at the top of all the streets: and they cast lots for her honorable men, and all her great men were bound in chains.--Nah. iii. 10.*

[12]Zech. xi. 5, &c.

*12 Whose possessors slay them, and hold themselves not guilty; and they that sell them say, Blessed be the Lord; for I am rich: and their own shepherds pity them not.--Zech. xi. 5.*

According to the letter and spirit of these passages, such treatment of human beings is deserving of death, though in some of them the same treatment is threatened as the punishment of the greatest sins, which amounts to the same thing, because human slavery is the living death and destruction of its victims--while in most of the same passages public destruction or national death is threatened, as the Divine retaliatory punishment for the public or customary practice of the same treatment, as their context clearly shows. Divine retaliatory punishment threatened in the Scriptures is generally of a similar kind to the national or public sins threatened.

IX. I lastly argue that the practice of human slavery is the identical crime of "man-stealing," from the nature of the practice itself, or the light in which the law of nature places it, as the highest species of larceny or theft that can be committed. Larceny, or stealing, in its most comprehensive sense, is the taking and withholding from one human being by another, of anything that justly belongs to the former, and to which and to its use the stealer or thief knows he has no just or moral right; the scriptural descriptions of crimes being far more comprehensive than our common law definitions of them, so as to correspond with the law of Nature in its requirements. By the will and gift of God every human being is, under God, the sole and exclusive owner of himself, and of all his own just rights, faculties and acquisitions. All these the slaveholder takes from his slaves, without any leave or licence from them, and without any compensation or equivalent, for his own exclusive use and benefit, just as the common thief steals common goods and chattels for his own exclusive use; both of these kinds of thieves well knowing they have no moral or just right to the property stolen, as each would instantly see and acknowledge, were the crime practiced upon himself. The slaveholder never pretends to take these things from third persons who are themselves left free, as the common thief does, and it is certain they are taken from the slaves without their leave. It is therefore larceny or stealing in fact, originating in the sin of covetousness, the same being the highest and most violent breach of the *eighth* and *tenth* commands of the decalogue, because the articles stolen are the most precious and valuable that men possess in this world, as uniform and universal experience testifies. None of the scriptural accounts of the crime of man-stealing describe it as the stealing of one person from another whose lawful property he was, but each of them, so far as it goes, describes it and its effects as the involuntary and forcible reduction of human beings to the condition of property, like other goods and chattels, and the use and treatment of them in that condition by means of criminal violence and fraud, exactly as slaves are now reduced to the same condition and subjected to the same use and treatment by the same criminal means. A careful examination and comparison of the numerous passages here quoted, will establish these facts clearly.

From the copious premises here quoted it is past all reasonable and honest doubt or controversy that human slavery is the same identical practice as the great crime of man-stealing, &c., so severely denounced and condemned in the Scriptures, that every slave-trader, purchaser, seller, slaveholder, and all persons engaged in the support of such slavery, such as slave overseers, and drivers, and persons engaged in the pursuit and capture of fugitive slaves, as well as those who legislate and otherwise act in favor of slavery, are deserving of the punishment of sure death by the Levitical or moral law, and that the communities and nations who tolerate and sanction the practice by law or custom, are obnoxious to the terrible retribution threatened as the punishment due to this great crime in the Scriptures.

Much quibbling is resorted to by the advocates of slavery on the subject of this alleged identity, on account of the pretended indefiniteness and obscurity with which the crime of "man-stealing," &c., is described in the Scriptures. But as I have already remarked, the scriptural descriptions are all more comprehensive than most human definitions are, so as to allow no chance for the guilty to escape. But it is necessary for me also to observe, that the scriptural descriptions of man-stealing, &c., are as plain as those of any other crime condemned in the Levitical law, and the identity of that crime with the practice of human slavery is as clearly exhibited in the Scriptures as the identity of murder, or any other crime condemned by that law, is with the crimes now supposed to be the same--so that if man-stealing, &c., be not the practice of slavery, so neither is the murder, mayhem, robbery, &c., described and condemned in the Scriptures, the same crimes which they are so currently supposed to represent in modern times. To those possessing "an honest and a good heart" (Luke xviii. 15), uncontaminated by the influence of slavery, no identity will naturally appear plainer, than that of man-stealing and human slavery, the reason why no such difficulty is experienced in identifying other crimes with those condemned in the Scriptures being, that the moral vision of most men is not obscured by their influence. But we should remember that this is a fearful subject wilfully to misunderstand or misinterpret, because the Scriptures assure us that if men do not become better they certainly grow worse by the exhibition of the true Gospel.

*2 Cor. ii 15, 16; iv. 3, 4, &c.*

I ought again to remark, in conclusion, that the customary cruelties, &c., which invariably attend the practice of human slavery, as absolutely necessary to its support and perpetuity, and therefore necessary incidents of the practice, are yet nowhere directly represented in the Scriptures as any part of the practice itself, which is both directly and indirectly described in the Scriptures as the conversion of human beings into property and nothing more.

# CHAPTER III.

## PERVERSIONS OF THE SCRIPTURES.

THOUGH plainly and severely as the practice of human slavery is thus condemned in the Scriptures, yet its advocates contend that the same practice is morally justified by them, thus making the word of God contradict itself, by first justifying and then condemning the same practice, at the same time and in the same code of laws!! But I have constantly observed that these advocates never attempt to point out and explain the specific distinction between these two cases, such for instance as those described in Ex. xxi. 2 and 16; the first of which is morally approved and justified because regulated by statute, while the other is morally condemned as one of the greatest crimes under the penalty of sure death. Nor do they ever attempt to settle the specific distinction between the acts described in Lev. xxv. 39, 47, and Deut. xxiv. 7, which are treated in the same manner in the Scriptures. They never tell us wherein the case recorded in Gen. xxvii. 12, 13, 23, 27, buying the services of men for a limited period, differs from that recorded in Gen. xxxvii. 27, 36, xlii. 21, 22, where Joseph was said to be sold or stolen; though it is equally plain that the first was approved, and the last condemned by God himself. They never attempt to reconcile these passages as describing the same subject, nor to point out the specific difference in their subjects, probably on account of the utter confusion in which the attempt would involve them. They never, in fact, mention the last quotations if they can avoid it, but content themselves with naked assertions that the first passages here quoted describe and justify the practice of human slavery. It becomes proper, therefore, to show at some length, that this doctrine of theirs is founded and sustained entirely on perversions of certain passages of the Scriptures, forged by falsifications of their true meaning and intent. Perversions of the Scriptures are a turning (perverto) of their true to a false meaning, and are denounced all over the Scriptures as among the greatest sins that men can commit, as indeed they necessarily must be, because they are attempts to make the Almighty say what He has not said, and to mean what He did not mean, to the destruction of human duty, rights, and happiness. Abolitionists have sometimes been severely censured for the moral severity with which they have condemned the pro-slavery perversions of the Scriptures, but let those who may feel disposed to repeat this censure read the following passages; Ps. cxix. 126; Isa. v., 20; Jer. xviii. 15, xxiii. 36; Eze. v. 6, 8, xiii. 9-16, xxii. 26, 28, xxxiv. 18, 19; Mic. iii. 9; Hab. i. 4; Zep. iii. 4; Mal. ii. 7, 8; Matt. xv. 3, 6, 9; Mark vii. 8; Acts xii. 10, xv. 1, 24; 2 Cor. ii. 17; Gal. i. 7; Col. ii. 8; 1 Pet. i. 18; 2 Pet. ii. 1; iii. 16; Rev. xxii. 18, 19, and numerous other similar passages.

It is proper here to add for the sake of perspicuity, that all the doctrines of the Scriptures are properly divisible into two kinds, namely: first, those which are matters of faith or belief only, and secondly, those that are matters of faith and practice both; the former being so indistinctly and obscurely revealed, that we may without any perversion or sin, honestly and innocently differ in opinion as to their true meaning, because we never can attain to absolute certainty with respect to many of their particulars; while the latter are so distinctly and clearly revealed, as the rules of our practice or practical duty, that there can be no honest or innocent difference of opinion respecting them. Of the former kind are the doctrines of the Creation, the fall of man, the Nature of Christ, the nature of Inspiration, the nature of the future state, &c. while of the latter kind are the rules of the Decalogue, the New Birth, the Law of Love, the

Golden Rule, and all other practical precepts of the Scriptures. The same distinction is made among the rules composing the great Law of Nature, though it is less obvious than the former. It is everywhere contended by the friends of the slave, that the Bible doctrines in relation to human slavery and its abolition belong entirely to the latter class, being so plainly and perspicuously revealed in the Scriptures, as to admit of *no honest difference of opinion* respecting them. They assert that any essential difference from their own opinions on those plain subjects, are evidence of rather a perverted heart in their adversaries, than of the incorrectness of those opinions. It is hoped that the following pages will clearly exhibit the truth of this assertion.

# CHAPTER IV.

## CASE OF CAIN.

THE absurd pro-slavery pretence that the people of Africa descended from Cain, and are included in the curse pronounced upon that murderer, would not be worth noticing were there not some few persons in the world, apparently weak, and stupid, and perverted enough, seriously to imagine its truth, as there is hardly anything in the world too absurd to be without some believers. That these people descended from Adam is certain. But as we find from [1]Gen. vii. 23, ix. 18, 19, and other passages, that they must have descended from Noah as well as from Adam, to settle the merits of this pretence we have only to ascertain whether Noah descended from Cain or not. From Gen. v. 3-32, we learn that Noah descended from Seth, another son of Adam, and a brother of Cain, a circumstance which renders it impossible for the latter to have had any descendants since the general deluge, or Noah's flood.

*1 And every living substance was destroyed which was upon the face of the ground, both man and cattle, and the creeping things, and the fowl of heaven; and they were destroyed from the earth; and Noah only remained alive, and they that were with him in the ark. And the sons of Noah that went forth of the ark, were Shem, and Ham, and Japheth; and Ham is the father of Canaan. These are the three sons of Noah: and of them was the whole earth overspread.--Gen. vii. 23; ix. 18, 19.*

As to the mark recorded in Gen. iv. 15, as having been put upon Cain, though some white people pretend it was the black color, the negroes retort that it was the white color, a controversy with which I feel no disposition to interfere.

# CHAPTER V.

# CASE OF CANAAN.[*]

**See Letter No. iv. of a series published by "A Disciple," in the Cincinnati Weekly Herald and Philanthropist," January, 1845.*

GREAT numbers of pro-slavery people contend that the negroes have descended from Canaan, the youngest son of Ham, who was cursed for his father's transgression, [1]-Gen. ix. 25-27, and that this curse was inflicted upon that race as his posterity. That this pretence is false in fact, I proceed next to show. As to Canaan himself, no part of the curse was ever inflicted upon him personally, so far as we know; for we have not only no account of any such infliction, but we learn from [2]Gen. x. 15-20,

*1 And he said, Cursed be Canaan; a servant of servants shall he be unto his brethren. And he said blessed be the Lord God of Shem; and Canaan shall be his servant. God shall enlarge Japheth, and he shall dwell in the tents of Shem; and Canaan shall be his servant.--Gen. ix. 25-27.*

*2 And Canaan begat Sidon his first-born, and Heth, and the Jebusite, and the Amorite, and the Girgasite, and*

*the Hivite, and the Arkite: and the Sinite, and the Arvadite, and the Zemarite, and the Hamathite: and afterward were the families of the Canaanites spread abroad. And the border of the Canaanites was from Sidon, as thou comest to Gerar, unto Gaza; as thou goest unto Sodom and Gomorrah, and Admah, and Zeboim, even unto Lasha. These are the sons of Ham, after their families, after their tongues, in their countries, and in their nations--Gen. x. 5-20.*

that he was the ancestor of whole tribes or nations of people apparently as free as others. The curse really was, however, afterwards inflicted on his posterity. To understand correctly when, and where, and how this was done, it is necessary to premise, that according to Gen. ix. 26, Canaan was to become subject to Shem--and that according to Gen. xi. 10-26, Abraham, the ancestor of the Ishmaelitish nation, descended from the latter--so that according to the true meaning of this prophetic curse, Canaan's posterity were to become subject to those of Shem--the Jews. According to Gen. x. 15, 19, xiii. 12, xv. 18, 21, xvii. 8 and other passages, the posterity of Canaan settled in that part of Asia then called the "Land of Canaan," the boundaries of which are well described and defined in the foregoing passages, from which we also learn, that God gave the same territory to Abraham and his posterity. But we have no account in the Scriptures, or in any other history, that any of the posterity of Canaan ever settled in Africa, nor have we any other evidence that any portion of the inhabitants of that continent could have descended from them, but the contrary, as will soon appear. We also learn from Num. xxiv. 2, 12, Josh. xii. 7, 8, and numerous other passages in the Pentateuch and the succeeding books, that this grant was actually fulfilled and carried into effect in the conquest of the "Land of Canaan" by the Jews, so that the curse pronounced upon Canaan was thus actually fulfilled, by his posterity the Canaanites thus becoming subject to those of Shem. No fulfilment of prophecy was ever plainer than this.

In Deut. xx. 10, 18, and other passages, the very mode of this fulfilment is described. Where the proof of the fulfilment of a prophecy is so very complete and satisfactory, it is useless to go into a long detail of other facts and circumstances still further to expose the falsity of the pretence under consideration. As the posterity of Canaan settled in Asia and not in Africa, there is not only no probability that the Africans descended from them, but the modern Syrians who did descend from them actually reside in Asia now, and are not negroes. The pretence is indeed surrounded with numerous other critical difficulties, such as that prophecies are not rules of moral duty or dispensations to commit sin, as numerous cases in the Scriptures prove, since the guilty agents of their fulfilment are there recorded as having been as surely punished as other sinners. See Matt. xviii. 7, xxvi. 24; Acts i. 16, 20; John xvii. 12; Rom. ix. 17, &c. That probably more of the posterity of Shem and Japhet, such as the ancient Greeks, and Romans, and modern English, Russians, Circassians, &c., have been enslaved or reduced to the condition of property than those of Ham have. But I forbear the critical exhibition of these numerous difficulties, because they have been sufficiently illustrated and explained by other writers, and because it is sufficient that I have proven the falsity of the pretence in point of fact. I ought to remark in conclusion, however, that the aboriginal inhabitants of Africa, and their present posterity, are supposed by the most approved antiquarians to have descended from Cush, Mizraim and Phut, the other three sons of Ham, upon whom no curse was pronounced. By these antiquarians Cush is supposed to have been the ancestor of the Ethiopian or negro portion, and Phut of the Carthaginian or Moorish portion, of the ancient and modern inhabitants of Africa. But be these conjectures as they may, it is certain that since the African posterity of these patriarchs have never yet been conquered and subjected in their own country, either by the descendants of Shem or by any others, if the curse pronounced upon Canaan was intended to attach to them or to their posterity, it remains thus far yet to be fulfilled. If, as some contend, the condition of enslavement be indicative of descent from Canaan, the rule will render a large portion of the present English and Americans such descendants, for it is only a few years since a multitude of their British ancestors were absolute slaves under the name of "villeins"-- also the same rule will render most of the present Russians, Poles, Georgians, Circassians, Turks, &c., lineal descendants of Canaan and Ham.

# CHAPTER VI.

## RULES OF CONSTRUCTION.

As in the investigation which is to follow, it will be necessary, in order to avoid perversion and ascertain the truth, to put different constructions on certain words and phrases, such as the subject matter and the context will clearly direct and require, it is proper here to specify certain rules of critical construction, which have been long since approved and universally adopted by critical commentators.

I. That the letter of a statute or other law be so construed, whenever it has different meanings in different uses and connections, as to harmonize with the spirit or general and collective meaning of the whole connection to which it belongs.

II. Where a double or different construction of the letter is admissible, that shall always be preferred which is most consistent with natural liberty, justice and righteousness, provided the general spirit of the law permit such construction.

III. All parts of every code or collection of laws or system of ethics are to be thus harmonized by construction, unless the express letter as well as the general spirit of the same prevent such harmony by such construction, in which case alone we are to allow that there is a conflict of laws in such code or collection. It is to be presumed that no fault will be found with these just and equitable rules, nor with their just and equitable application to the present important subject matter *now under consideration.*

# CHAPTER VII.

## USES OF THE WORDS "BUY" AND "SELL."

MULTITUDES of pro-slavery advocates contend, that because the words "buy" and "sell" are used in describing some of the customary legal Hebrew servitudes, the latter must necessarily have been slavish, and such seems to be the general belief or impression even among preachers of the gospel and professors of religion. But this proposition must as a certain and infallible rule necessarily be false, because the same words are oftener used in the Scriptures to describe free and voluntary service, than they are to describe slavish service or slavery. Thus, in such passages as Gen. xxxvii. 27, 28, 36; Ex. xxi. 16; Deut. xxiv. 7, &c., they are undoubtedly used to describe the condition of slavery, while in Gen. xlvii. 19-23; 1 Kings xxi. 20, 25; 2 Kings xvii. 17; Isa. l. 1, lii. 3; Acts xx. 28; Rom. vii. 14; 1 Cor. vi. 20, vii. 23; 2 Pet. ii. 1, &c., the same words are just as certainly used to describe free and voluntary service, as their context clearly proves, and as is universally admitted among Bible commentators and critics. So sensible are the advocates of slavery of the truth of these propositions, that they never dare to compare such cases as those contained in Gen. xxxvii. and xlvii., in Ex. xxi. 2-16, and Deut. xv. 12, and xxiv. 7; because if they admit a difference between them, that difference can only be the same as between free service and slavery, *which contradicts and ruins the whole theory of Bible slavery*; while if they assert the identity of the practices described, the ready inquiry instantly occurs, why did God, who never does anything in vain, regulate and thereby approve and sanction a practice in the passages first quoted, but condemn it in those last quoted under the penalty of death? This inquiry is so distressing to the advocates of slavery that they always avoid it if possible by neglecting and refusing to notice such passages as Gen. xxxvii. 27, 28, 36; Ex. xxi. 16; Deut. xxiv. 7; 1 Tim. i. 9, 10, and other passages which describe and condemn such slavery as one of the greatest crimes or violations of the moral law; but simply content themselves with obstinately asserting, that the passages describing the Patriarchal and Hebrew servitudes where these words "buy" and "sell" are used, describe slavery and nothing else.

But from the foregoing clear premises we discover, that from the mere scriptural use of these words alone in describing the condition of servitude or service, nothing can certainly be determined respecting its real nature, which, as in every similar case of critical doubt and construction, is to be ascertained, determined, and understood, by the subject matter, by the context, and by the general description or spirit of each passage, all taken in connection with the letter or language thereof. Such, when we are honest, is always our customary mode of examination or reasoning. Thus no person supposes from the description given in 1 Kings xxi. 20, 25, that Ahab was a slave or article of personal property, because we see from the context of his life, actions, and character recorded in the same and other books, that he was a king and absolute monarch. So no person supposes from the description in such passages as Acts xx. 28; Rom. vii. 14; 1 Cor. vi. 20, vii. 23; 2 Pet. ii. 1, that Paul and his converts were property or slaves, because the context describes them as free and voluntary servants of Christ. In a similar manner, though slaveholders customarily call their slaves their "servants," yet we know them to be slaves from the circumstances in which the word is used. On the contrary, in England and other free countries, we know the persons customarily called "servants" are not property or slaves, from the circumstances attending the customary use of the same word. It will no doubt be said in reply to these observations, that these words are employed in the passages here quoted in a typical or figurative sense merely, and do not in that sense mean slavish service or slavery. THIS PROPOSITION IS TRUE. In the passages under consideration these words are used in a typical or figurative sense, as descriptive of free and voluntary service only. But the important inquiry immediately arises, where are the types or figures from which these free descriptions are copied to be found? For it should be specially noticed and remembered, that these types must have existed before the descriptions did, and been free also, because a free description can no more be taken from a slave type, than a slavish description can from a free type--every typical description in the Scriptures corresponds in its nature with its type. I answer, that the types or figures here sought after are these same Patriarchal and Hebrew servitudes, the nature of which is so much controverted, because all the types referred to in the New Testament are contained in the Levitical law and the lives of the Patriarchs, and nowhere else, and no other types suited to these descriptions except servitudes are to be found in either. But as these descriptions are all free, so these typical servitudes from which they are copied must have been free also. According to the descriptive testimony of the New Testament, therefore, all those servitudes were free and voluntary, and both Testaments thus far completely harmonized.

Nothing in this plain and decisive testimony ought to surprise us as strange or uncommon, because we ourselves, in common with the people of most other modern nations, customarily and familiarly use the same words "buy" and "sell" to describe free and voluntary service. Thus, we customarily say with respect to town or parish paupers, that they are "to be sold." We always customarily mean thereby, that their support and maintenance are to be sold to the lowest bidder. So we say figuratively from custom respecting poor foreign immigrants, that they are "sold," or that they "sell themselves" to pay for their passages. We always customarily and really mean by these expressions that they agree beforehand to let themselves out to labor after their arrival, in payment of the money advanced by their employers to pay for their passage; it being especially to be noticed in this connection and remembered by the reader, that the immigrants in this case receive the pay for the labor *before* the same is to be performed. With a similar meaning we customarily say of venal politicians, that they "sell themselves," and are "bought" or "purchased" by their employers or patrons--nobody being in the least deceived in any of these cases by the use of this phraseology, into a false belief that slavish service was intended by it, or that the kinds of service described were not entirely free and voluntary. So where people are deceived and their interests betrayed by their representatives or public confidential agents, the same kind of phraseology is sometimes employed the more forcibly to express the baseness of the supposed treachery, or the greatness of the injury sustained. The histories of the revolution tell us that Benedict Arnold was "bought" by British gold, and that Williams, Paulding and Van Wart could not be bought by Major André. When a northern clergyman marries a rich southern widow, country gossip thus hits off the indecency: "The cotton bags *bought* him." Sir Robert Walpole said, "every man has his price, and whoever will pay it, can *buy* him," and John Randolph said, "The Northern delegation is in the market; give me money enough and I can *buy* them." The temperance publications tell us that candidates for office *buy* men with whiskey. The same, or corresponding words and phrases, are employed for various purposes in other parts of the Scriptures, but generally to describe certain other free and voluntary customs of the ancient oriental nations. See Gen. xxix. 15-29, xxxiv. 11, 12; Ex. xx. 7, 11, xxii. 17, xxxiv. 20; Lev. xxvii. 2-8; Numb. xviii. 15, 16; Deut. xxii. 28, 29; Judg. i. 12, 13, ii. 14, iii. 8, iv. 2; Ruth iv. 10; 1 Sam. xviii. 25, 27; Hosea iii. 2, &c. I shall hereafter have occasion to remark upon the nature of the ancient Hebrew free custom, of buying and "selling" Hebrew wives, wards, and children.

# CHAPTER VIII.

## THE TRUE ISSUE.

FROM the premises already stated it clearly appears that TWO ENTIRELY DIFFERENT MODES OR WAYS of buying and selling people, the one free and voluntary, and the other slavish, are plainly described in the Scriptures as having been in customary use among the ancients, just as they now are among the moderns. The real controversy between the Bible advocates of slavery and their opponents then is as follows, namely: Were the ancient Patriarchal and Hebrew servitudes in controversy, slavish or otherwise? Were Abraham's servants, said to have been "bought with his money," free servants or slaves? Were the Levitical servants who were said to "sell themselves," and to be bought by their masters, and to be "their money," free and voluntary servants, or were they slaves and property? These important inquiries form the only material issue now in controversy, and since it has been shown that the mere scriptural employment and use of the foregoing words and phrases proves nothing definite and certain in relation to it, and does nothing towards settling the merits of the controversy, the same must be decided and determined as in other similar cases, by the subject matter of the narrative, by the context, and by the whole general description of the actual condition of those servants, all taken in connection with those words and phrases. Several other subordinate controverted matters will arise for consideration in our progress, such as, Whether the Levitical law justified any form or degree of human oppression? Whether the Holy Prophets did the same? Whether Christ and his Apostles connived at and sanctioned heathen Greek and Roman slavery? &c. But the principal true material issue attending the whole controversy is that above stated.

# CHAPTER IX.

## KEY TO THE INQUIRY.

PREPARATORY to the further investigation of this important subject, it is proper for the reader to understand and become skilled in the use of what I call the *Key to the Inquiry*, which said "Key" consists in the critical examination and comparison of several passages in the Scriptures, in which the foregoing words and phrases are used to describe two different kinds of human service, a few specimens of which are as follows. The first specimen is the comparison of Gen. xvii. 12, 13, 23, 27, with Acts xx. 28; 1 Cor. vi. 20, vii. 23. In each of these cases the servants are said to have been "bought," or "purchased" (and of course were "sold")--in the first case "with money," and in the other "with blood," and "with a price." By any rule of critical reasoning or construction whatever, if the mere use of those words and phrases alone is to decide that Abraham and the other Patriarchs were slaveholders, then the same use decides that Christ and his Apostles were slaveholders also, owning and treating their own converts as property or slaves, and possessing the equal character and qualities of slaveholders both ancient and modern, as much as Abraham and the other Patriarchs can be supposed to have done. Thus if it be argued that property is commonly "bought" with property, and that "money" is property, so also is "blood" and "a price," property in common estimation, as much so as money is. But the supposition or notion of our Saviour and his Apostles being slaveholders, and their converts being their slaves, is too absurd and wicked for intelligent belief. This specimen is therefore a comparison of free service with free service, which is so much plainer as the one kind was the type of the other.

The second specimen is the critical comparison of the case recorded in Gen. xxxvii. 28, 36, with that recorded in Gen. xlvii. 19, 26, as follows:

From the human sale recorded in Gen. xxxvii., we learn the following particulars.

1st. That the person sold (Joseph) was thus treated without his consent and against his will.

2d. That he was no party to the bargain or contract by which he was sold, any more than a beast or other article of property is.

3d. That he received no part of the price, consideration or compensation (twenty pieces of silver), for which he was sold, any more than a beast or other article of property does.

4th. That the effect of the sale was to convert him into an article of property, as suitable for subsequent traffic and merchandise in, as beasts and other kinds of property are.

5th. That according to Gen. xlii. 21, 22, this transaction is represented to have been so great a crime or sin, as to be deserving of death by the laws of nature.

From the human sale recorded in Gen. xlvii., we learn,

1st. That the persons sold (the Egyptians) were thus treated at their own earnest request.

2d. That they "sold themselves," and alone made the whole contract with the purchaser.

3d. That they themselves received the whole of the price, consideration or compensation (support during the years of famine) given on the contract for their sale.

4th. That the effect of the whole transaction was to render them tenants at a very reasonable rent, but otherwise to leave them just as free in all other respects as they were before.

5th. That according to the Scripture account of it, the whole transaction was perfectly moral and virtuous in its own nature, and just as free and equal as common leasing and hiring now are.

Here then are two scriptural accounts in the same book, of two different purchases and sales of human beings, both entirely opposite to each other in their moral and political nature, effects and consequences. In the first case, the word "sold" is used, and "bought" understood, because there cannot be a sale without a purchase. While in the second, the word "bought" is used, and "sold" understood, because there cannot be a purchase without a "sale." This specimen then is a comparison of a slave sale, with a voluntary sale of free service. The critical reader will also remark that in the latter case quoted from Gen. xlvii., the Egyptians who "sold themselves" received their pay *before* their services were to commence or be rendered, just as poor foreigners said to be "sold to pay their passage" receive it now; whereas the "hired servants" mentioned in the Levitical law did not receive their pay until *after* their work was performed, as most hirelings now do, which is the only material distinction made in the Scriptures between bought and hired servants, both kinds being in all other respects equally free, voluntary and privileged. We make the same necessary inference respecting the payment of the ancient "bought" Hebrew servants, from the descriptions contained in such passages as Lev. xxvi. 49; Neh. v. 5, &c. We also infer that these bought servants might freely hold property of their own, a right wholly incompatible with the condition of slavery. From Lev. xxv. 47; Neh. v. 8, &c., we also learn that this free custom of purchasing servants of themselves in payment of previous debts contracted by them, was general throughout the ancient oriental countries.

The last specimen I shall offer is the critical comparison of Ex. xxi. 16, and Deut. xxiv. 7, with 1 Kings xxi. 20, 25; 2 Kings xvii. 17; Isa. l. 1, lii. 3; Rom. vii. 14; 2 Pet. ii. 1-3, &c., by which, from the light furnished by the comparison just made, similar inferences will be easily and readily drawn; the same being also a comparison of slave kidnapping, and slave selling and holding, with free and voluntary service figuratively described. From the descriptions in the passages quoted it is certain, that neither King Ahab, nor the Jews, nor the Apostles Paul and Peter, and their converts therein mentioned, could have been property or slaves, in any respect or sense whatever. See John viii. 33; Gal. iv. 1. It is proper for the sake of perspicuity again to repeat the remark that the only important scriptural distinction made between bought and sold servants, and hired servants, is as follows: namely, when their wages or pay were advanced to them beforehand, they were said to "sell themselves" and to be "bought" by their creditors or employers to repay the same, as the examples already quoted clearly prove. But where the wages or pay were not to be received till the labor was performed, the Hebrew servants were said to be "hired," as we see in Deut. xxiv. 15, and many similar passages.

But excepting this one mere nominal distinction, and that of the heritable disability of foreign servants, to be noticed hereafter, not another can be found in the Scriptures, in the equal rights and privileges of these two classes, of Hebrew and other ancient oriental servants.

# CHAPTER X.

## PRO-SLAVERY PERVERSIONS OF THE OLD TESTAMENT.

### Examination of Gen. xii. 5; xvii. 12, 13, 23, 27; xx. 14; xxiv. 35.

From the strong light furnished by the copious premises already stated, the remainder of our task will be comparatively easy. The Hebrew word *Quanah* so frequently rendered "buy" in the common English translation of the Old Testament, is literally rendered "gotten" in Gen. xii. 5, as it should be in some other passages where it is rendered "buy." The word literally means to get, gain, acquire, procure, obtain, possess; but it is more frequently used in the Scriptures than the word *Kaurau*, which literally means to buy or purchase. From the phrase "souls that they had gotten," which occurs in this passage, the advocates of slavery infer that Abraham's servants were slaves. But I agree in opinion with Mr. Dickey, that these "souls" were the converts which Abraham had made to the true religion--especially as this construction harmonizes with Abraham's history and character-- and with the spirit of the

Scriptures. From the expression used in Gen. xvii. 12, 13, 23, 27, the same pro-slavery inference is customarily drawn. But as we have seen that the scriptural use of these words and phrases does not necessarily describe the condition of slavery, we are obliged to resort to the context to discover the real condition of Abraham's servants. The amount of the evidence thus furnished is small, and entirely circumstantial, but that little is very strong. From these same verses it appears that the same religious rights and privileges were secured to Abraham's servants, that belonged to him and his own children; a strong analogical proof that they shared all other rights, because real slaves have no rights whatever, and it is not likely that these servants would be allowed some rights equally with children, but be denied all others.

From Gen. xx. 7, we learn that Abraham was a prophet. From Gen. xii. 7, 8, xiii. 4, and other passages, that he was a priest-- and from Gen. xxiii. 6, that he was a "mighty prince," or king--he being in each of these three offices the type of Christ,-- From Gen. xiii. 2, xxiv. 35, and other passages, that he was very wealthy and powerful. From such passages as Gen. xiv. 22, 23, xviii. 18, 19, &c., we learn, that he was equally remarkable for natural honesty, justice, equity and righteousness.

It also appears from Gen. xii. 1-37, xv. 1-18, xvii. 1-22, xviii. 1, 13, 17, &c., that he had frequent visions from God, that the greatest Divine promises were made to him and his posterity, and that he enjoyed more of the Divine favor than any other person of his time. What probability is there that such a character as this would have been guilty of a practice afterwards condemned in the Scriptures under the penalty of death, both by the laws of Nature and Revelation? Not the slightest whatever. Were it not for the wickedness involved in it, nothing can be conceived more ludicrously amusing, than the notion of Father Abraham buying and selling slaves, feeding them on a peck of corn a week, selling fathers from their children, husbands from their wives, or exhibiting conduct in an other respect resembling that of our modern professed Christian slaveholders. It would be just as absurd and unreasonable to suppose that Christ and his Apostles were guilty of such conduct, as that Abraham was, the wickedness being no greater in the one case than in the other. What is there recorded in the lives and characters of the other patriarchs, that could induce us to suspect that they might have been slaveholders?

From the information given in Gen. vi. 5-13, it is highly probable that the antediluvians were destroyed for the crime of slavish violence among other sins. But there is no probability that Noah, who with his family alone were saved on account of his justice and righteousness (see Gen. vi. 8, 9, vii. 1, &c.), would afterwards have been guilty of the same sinful practice that destroyed the rest. Nor is there any probability that such righteous persons as Isaac, and Jacob, and the other patriarchs are described to have been, would have been customarily guilty of a practice so utterly repugnant to the Law of Nature as human slavery is. As that practice is described in the Scriptures, Gen. xlii. 21, 22, as being utterly condemned by that great law, there cannot be the slightest reason to suppose that any of the patriarchs adopted it--for God certainly would never have selected as the chosen depositories of the true religion, persons who were in the habit of violating it without scruple or remorse, especially in acts that were afterwards condemned by express revelation to be punished with *death*; for slavery is as great and as plain a crime against natural as revealed religion, as the last argument, or subjection to the condition of slavery, will immediately convince the most inveterate friend of human slavery. It should be remembered, however, that as the patriarchs lived under the dim and uncertain light of the Law of Nature, they like Joseph's brethren occasionally fell into great errors and sins, of which from the bad consequences they had frequent occasions for repentance, whether they improved them or not--so that even if under this dim light they had committed the sin of slavish oppression, their conduct in that respect would have been no more moral example or justification of our own, than that of Joseph's brethren in selling him was.

A pro-slavery quibble has been raised from the descriptions contained in such passages as Gen. xiii. 2, 24, xxxv. 30, 43, &c., that Abraham's servants must have been slaves, because they are mentioned in connection with beasts and other property. But if this mode of reasoning be correct, then according to Gen. xii. 5, Abraham's wife Sarah, and Lot his nephew, must have been his slaves also. So according to Ex. xx. 17, and v. 21, all wives must have been slaves or property. Nay, further, from the words in the command, "*nor anything that is thy neighbor's,*" it appears that all the husbands, parents, children, and other relations, comprising in fact the whole Israelitish nation, must have been slaves! But under such strange circumstances the material inquiry instantly occurs, where did they all find masters? So according to the same logic we see from Job i. 3, 4; xlii. 12, 13, that Job's wife and children must have been his slaves. Our common law must also render all servants under its jurisdiction slaves, because it gives precisely the same remedies to masters for injuries done to their servants, that it does to their beasts and other property. So where a nation acquires new territory by treaty or otherwise, it must by the law of nations sustain the same relation to the inhabitants of the territory, that it does to the territory itself, and as the latter is property the former must be property also. But enough of these absurd consequences in reply to nonsense. The pro-slavery mistake is made by confounding the relations of persons with those of things, merely because the latter happen to be mentioned in connection with the former, while it always appears from the whole context, describing the condition of the ancient Hebrew servants, that by the gift or transfer of persons and property in the same transaction, the opposite relations previously existing between them and the donors were not altered as between them and the donors. This case finely illustrates the sophistry which relates a part of a narrative or story only, the effect of which is often the same as telling a fasehood--as by means of it we are able to prove from the Scriptures themselves, that there is no God. See Ps. xiv. 1; liii. 1, &c.

# CHAPTER XI.

## PRO-SLAVERY PERVERSIONS OF THE OLD TESTAMENT.

## Examination of Ex. xii. 43, 45; xx. 17; xxi. 2-6, 7, 11, 20, 21; Deut. xv. 12-18; xxi. 10, 14.

It is not to be supposed that after the lapse of so many thousand years, we can now fully understand the exact nature of the customary ancient Hebrew servitudes which in some way were so different from our own. Nor is it to be expected that we can now fully understand the exact intended application of all the short political as well as moral statutes in the Levitical Law. Like other very ancient writings, much obscurity must rest and remain on most of them. They were evidently intended to regulate and restrain the ancient legal customs which then prevailed among the Israelites, probably in common with all the other ancient oriental nations--these statutes holding a similar relation to those customs, that our modern national and state constitutions do to our other laws and customs--while a critical examination of the same statutes shows that the spirit if not the letter of them is just as useful now as it ever was, to regulate, and restrain, and guide all human legislation--no other laws now existing being so perfectly adapted to secure the temporal as well as spiritual happiness of mankind as those contained in the ancient Levitical code.

It appears from the statute in Ex. xii. 43, 45, that though servants "bought for money" could eat the passover after they had been circumcised, yet neither strangers nor foreigners, nor hired servants were permitted to eat it, so that since these bought servants were allowed a greater privilege than hired servants and strangers were, we may safely conclude without further comment, that this was a case of the free and voluntary sale of such servants by themselves. We see from the 48th and 49th verses of the same chapter, that no legal distinctions were made by the Levitical law, between the rights of strangers and native Israelites, as they were to be governed by the same laws, and the phrase "*he shall be as one born in the land,*" also proving that after circumcision these adopted foreigners were as much "brethren" and "children of Israel" as the native Jews were--a rule well worthy of the consideration of those who are in favor of disfranchising foreigners. It should be further remarked that under one single code of laws intended to govern all the individuals in a nation, it is impossible to make any distinction in the natural rights of those individuals, or any of them. As Dr. Duncan⁻*

*In a work of 136 pages by the Rev. James Duncan, the father of the Hon. Alexander Duncan, Member of Congress from Cincinnati, first published at Vevay, Ia., 1824, and republished by the American Anti-slavery society, 1840.*

long since observed, it is certainly a very strange circumstance that the tenth commandment  (Ex. xx. 17; Deut. v. 21, &c.) should ever have been pressed into the service of human slavery, because that practice is a direct violation or breach of this as well as of the eighth commandment--it being impossible for one person to enslave another, without first "coveting," or eagerly desiring what he knows is not morally and justly his own--and cannot therefore morally and justly belong to him, as he himself would instantly see and acknowledge, were he himself, or his family, or friends, to be themselves enslaved. This command being then a direct condemnation of human slavery, it is most wickedly absurd to quote the same in its defence when it can only be honestly quoted for its condemnation. I have already sufficiently illustrated the other absurd consequences that result from this wicked pro-slavery perversion.

The statutes in Ex. xxi. 2-6, and Deut. xv. 12-18, limit the voluntary sales of native Hebrew servants for the payment of their debts, to the period of six years at a time. While it appears from Lev. xxv. 44-46, and other passages, that adopted foreign servants might sell themselves for still longer periods, even up to the Jubilee. The political reason or policy of this distinction was, that foreigners could not hold real estate in the nation any longer than the Jubilee, when all the land in the country reverted back to its original owners or their heirs (see Lev. xxv. 10-13, &c.), so that as poor foreign immigrants into the nation could seldom obtain any land at all, it would frequently be more convenient for them to contract for periods of service longer than six years, though none were permitted to extend beyond the Jubilee. In Ex. xxi. 2, the description is, "if thou buy (procure) a Hebrew servant," &c.--but by whom and of whom is not said. The proper inquiry therefore is, did Hebrew servants of this description "sell themselves" as free and voluntary servants, as the

Egyptians did to Joseph? Or were they sold by third persons to others as slaves, as Joseph was by his brethren to the Ishmaelite's? for the words "buy" and "sell" prove nothing either way. So far as we now know anything about the mode of sales of service, the servants certainly "sold themselves" (Gen. xlvii. 19, 23; Lev. xxv. 47) by free and voluntary contract, just as poor foreign immigrants are now sometimes said to do. The use of the words and phrases here alluded to proves nothing against this mode, because a person who "sells himself" is still "bought" and "sold" just as the Egyptians were when they sold themselves to Joseph to be Pharaoh's servants. Besides, were this statute intended to regulate slave sales, there is no probability that they would have been limited to the period of six years, but would have been in perpetuity like the sales of other property. For these reasons the statute was undoubtedly intended to regulate free and voluntary service. But it appears from the whole statute (Ex. xxi. 2-6), that though these sales were free and voluntary as well as limited, yet they might in one case be extended by an addition to the original contract. To understand the true meaning of the transaction we must recollect, that it was limited to the case of marriage by the servant during his term. The wife being a servant as well as the husband, when her term of service extended beyond his, he would be separated from his family, if he left his master's service at the expiration of his own term. If in those circumstances he wished to remain longer in service, the policy of the statute was to render the new contract a public legal transaction, and matter of legal record, so that the master should take no advantage of his superior power to oppress the servant therein, the Hebrew legal custom of boring the ear being used by the judges to ratify it. While it is at the same time perfectly clear from the language of the statute, that to the last transaction, whatever the first was, the servant was a free and voluntary party; so that if he became a slave for life, as many pretend he did, he did so by his own free choice and request; while if his family were slaves also, he must have been excessively foolish to have become so for the sake of living with them, when the master might lawfully sell and separate them from him at any time, just as our modern slaveholders do. The Almighty never enacted a law to sanction such absurdity as this, because he never does anything in vain.

The statutes now under consideration, Ex. xxi. 2-6; Deut. xv. 12-18, were evidently enacted for the special benefit of the servant and not of the master. The length of time the former was bound to serve under the new contract is translated "for ever" in the common English Bible, which is doubtless an incorrect literal translation. The two Hebrew words in most common use to express general terms or periods of time are "*Edh*" and "*olaum*" the exact ancient use and meaning of which it is not certain we now know. All that we now certainly know about them is, that "*Edh*" means time certain, fixed, and definite, while "*olaum*" (alone used in these statutes) means time unseen, hidden, and indefinite, probably nearly the same as our English words "ever" and "always," and is certainly used in the Scriptures in a manner nearly as indefinite as we use these adverbs.

When these two words are used together they are commonly translated "for ever," "everlasting," "eternal," &c., as "olaum" sometimes is when used alone, though they never literally mean thus, except when the subject matter admits of eternal duration. But as it always means a period or term of some kind, we are left to conjecture what that was in these statutes. It is ridiculous to understand it to mean eternal duration in them, because the period or term of service could not extend beyond the natural lives of the servant and his family, and by the same code of laws no servant could serve as such beyond the Jubilee. The period really intended by the statutes must therefore be ascertained by their object, which was in the case of the new contract, to prevent the separation of servants from their families. Judging from this object and from the fact that some finite period or term of time must have been intended, the most reasonable and satisfactory construction or explanation is, that it was the unexpired balance of the wife's term, which might extend to the Jubilee, but never in any case beyond it. This construction is the most likely to be correct, and it is the more just and conclusive, as it corresponds with the spirit of the Scriptures, and harmonizes the latter, while any other construction is almost sure to confuse them. The statutes provided in Ex. xxi. 7-11, and Deut. xxi. 10, 14, were made to regulate the well known oriental custom of buying and selling daughters and female wards for wives. Contrary to our own custom in such cases, by which parents and guardians give portions, dowries, or endowments to their daughters and female wards when they marry, and which usually becomes the property of their husbands; ancient oriental husbands, when they married, gave the parents or guardians of their wives the same consideration or compensation, and were thus said to "buy" or "purchase," and the parents or guardians to "sell" them their wives-- the whole custom being just as free and equal or equitable as our own is. In this way Jacob purchased his two wives by fourteen years of hard labor. Gen. xxix. 15-20. Several other examples of the same custom are recorded in the Scriptures, see Gen. xxiv. 4, 22, 38, 48, 51, 53; Deut. xxii. 28, 29; Judg. i. 12, 13; Ruth iv. 10; 1 Sam. xviii. 25, 27; Hos. iii. 2, &c. The statute in Ex. xxi. 7, 11, is somewhat obscure, but seems to have been intended for the case of betrothal before marriage, agreeably to the oriental custom here alluded to, and was made to prevent the abuse of that custom. As her intended husband had paid the customary dowry for her, the custom probably allowed him to receive it back from any other preferred suitor; but if she had none such, and he still refused to marry her, the statute gave it to her as reasonable damages for his violation of the contract. So if he had purchased her for one of his sons, but refused to complete the contract by actual marriage, the statute gave her the same measure of damages.

By the statute in Deut. xxi. 10, 14, the husband was allowed the right of voluntary divorce, if he became dissatisfied with his heathen wife--but as he had given no dowry or sum to obtain her, it was unreasonable he should obtain one after he had divorced her, and as he would be sure to injure her by the divorce, this statute wisely provided that no pecuniary consideration or temptation should ever be allowed to influence the transaction, so that although the divorced woman might afterwards marry again, the first husband should derive no benefit from her second marriage. As the Scriptures everywhere encourage matrimony for the gratification of honest love, they permitted it in this case for that purpose even between true believers and heathens, but allowed this voluntary divorce as a remedy for the evil consequences that would sometimes be likely to ensue from such unions. It is very remarkable, that in this case and that in 1 Cor. vii. 15, heathenism was permitted to be a sufficient cause for voluntary divorce, because according to Eph. ii. 15; iv. 18, &c., heathen persons are considered as spiritually dead, and as such most dangerous companions to true believers, from which doctrine most Christian legislators have perhaps correctly inferred, that where Christian husbands and wives behave like heathen, or perhaps worse than heathen, as by long wilful absence, by extreme cruelty, gross neglect, base fraud, &c., the same conduct ought, addition to adultery, to be sufficient causes of divorce to the injured party.

Ex. xxi. 20, 21, is a statute regulating a peculiar case of homicide which would be liable to great abuse without such a regulation. As the oriental custom in common with that allowed masters to give their servants necessary and reasonable correction the same as to children (see Deut. viii. 5; Prov. iii. 12, xiii. 24, xix. 18, xxiii. 13, 14, xxix. 15, 17; Heb. xii. 7, 9, &c.), to prevent the abuse of this right the statute declared it to be what we call manslaughter, and subjected the master to the vengeance of the relations of the deceased servant, to kill a servant during his chastisement, even with the ordinary instrument of punishment, a provision that never would have been enacted had Hebrew servants been the lawful property of their masters; because every man might then, as he may now, lawfully slaughter his beasts, and destroy his other property at his own discretion, provided that in so doing he do not infringe the rights of others, which could not in this case be done to the servants if they were slaves, because the latter could have no rights to infringe.

The Hebrew text of the 20th verse literally reads, "he shall surely be avenged," probably meaning thereby that the relations of the deceased servant might kill the master, provided they could overtake him before he reached a city of refuge, agreeably to the statutes recorded in Num. xxxv. 14-21, 30, 32; Deut. xix. 2-7, 11-13; Josh. xx. 2, 9, &c. Some are of opinion, from the great strength of the expression here quoted, that the master, in case of the immediate death of the servant, was to be punished as a murderer, even though he reached a city of refuge. But however this might have been, in order to prevent the abuse of the statute itself, it was provided in the 21st verse, that if the servant did not immediately die from the chastisement, that circumstance, together with the fact that it was for the master's interest to preserve the life of the servant, should be sufficient presumptive evidence of accidental death, that the master had no murderous intent, and that he ought not therefore to be punished at all. It is my opinion that the phrase "for he is his money," applies equally to both of these verses, and was intended as the special reason why, as the master was interested to preserve the life of the servant, he ought not to be held guilty of murder, in either of these cases of homicide. It is also certain that this very phrase is even now sometimes used in a free sense, being borrowed perhaps from this very statute--a statute provided for the special benefit and protection of both masters and servants in a case which would be liable to the greatest abuse without it, from the extreme irritation produced by such transactions-- all other cases of murder, maim, and other abuses of servants by their masters, being regulated by the statutes against those crimes, see Ex. xxi. 12-14, 26, 27, 32, &c. It is proper to remark in this connection that though the oriental custom permitted parents, as we have seen, to chastise their children with the same instrument, yet no similar statute was provided in the Levitical law, for the homicide of children by their parents. The reason of this omission was the presumption that the natural affection of the latter would always prevent that crime, but which would be wanting sufficiently to protect the rights of servants, and prevent the abuse of the same by their masters without the assistance of special legislation.

# CHAPTER XII.

## PRO-SLAVERY PERVERSIONS OF THE OLD TESTAMENT.

### Examination of Lev. xxv. 39-43, 44-46, 47-54.

Lev. xxv. 39-43, and 47-54, are other Levitical statutes regulating the voluntary sales of free Hebrew servants, made for the payment of their debts previously contracted, as is evident from the statutes themselves, and as has been sufficiently illustrated and explained. This fact appears very plainly from the latter statute, and from the 25th to the 32d verses of the same chapter, where the redemption provided for would be impossible and absurd, were they not for the payment of such debts; for it is certain that the servants "sold themselves," which they could not have done without payment, which they must have received at or before the time of their sales, for otherwise they would have nothing to redeem themselves for or from after sale. It also appears from these "redemptions" that these "sold" and "bought" servants must have been in debt to or owed their masters, which they could not have done had they been slaves, any more than beasts or other lawful property could. They were therefore all free and voluntary servants. We see also from these statutes that foreigners settled in the nation had the same customary right to purchase native servants, that the native Israelites themselves had. But in the latter case the servants might be redeemed at any time by the payment of the debts they had sold themselves for, and as (v. 49) the servants might if they were able redeem themselves, this very fact also proves that they could not be property or slaves, because no slave has a right to property, and can acquire none but what belongs to his master. The same statutes taken in connection with the 10th and 13th verses of the chapter also prove, that the contract for these voluntary sales could last only till the next Jublilee, when all poor servants were not only discharged from such contracts, but the native servants were restored to the possession of their paternal inheritance or estates.

A multitude of laws have been contrived in the world, to prevent the suffering and oppression of the poor and the helpless, but the whole of them put together are but trifles for that purpose, when compared with the statutes embodied in the Levitical law, and especially those contained in

Leviticus xxv., for it was impossible for much oppression of the poor to exist where these regulations were faithfully observed, it being only where they were disregarded and violated that such oppression was ever complained of among the Jews, see Neh. v. 1-13; Jer. xxxiv. 8, 22, &c. Multitudes of persons, including many professed preachers of the gospel, seriously contend that the Scriptures do not teach politics or political matters at all. But the single statute in Lev. xxv. 8-15, providing for the great institution of the Jubilee, had a more extensive and abiding political effect, and produced more extensive political as well as moral consequences, than the whole of the political measures heretofore made the objects of party strife in the United States put together. The statutes under consideration and others of a similar character interspersed throughout the Levitical law (see Ex. xxii. 21-27, xxiii. 9; Lev. xix. 33, 34, xxv. 35-37; Deut. xv. 7, 11, &c.), also exhibit the extreme care and tenderness manifested in that law, for the support and protection of the poor, and needy, and helpless, and especially for poor foreigners and strangers. No such statutes are provided in this code for the protection of the wealthy and powerful, and their usurped rights, as abound in most human codes, for the very sufficient reason that the rich need no such protection under that or any other righteous code. I hold it to be the height of wickedness to pretend that such a code as this was intended to sanction such a practice as human slavery.

Preparatory to a critical examination of the celebrated statute contained in Lev. xxv. 44-46, it will be necessary to correct the common English translation of it, the same being the falsest translation I ever saw. The exact literal translation of it is as follows: verse 44--"And thy man servant, and thy maiden, which shall be to thee (shall be) from the nations which surround you. From them shall ye procure (the) man servant and the maiden."

Verse 45. "And also from the sons of the foreigners, the strangers among you, from them shall ye procure--and from their families which (are) among you, which they brought forth into your land, and (they) shall be to you for a possession."

Verse 46. "And ye shall possess them yourselves for your sons after you, for to possess (as) a possession. For ever of them shall ye serve yourselves. And over your brethren the sons of

Israel, man towards his brother, thou shalt not rule over with rigor."

This is as exact a literal translation of the statute as can be made, though the phraseology of it may be so varied in several instances, as to read in a more elegant English idiom, without any alteration or variation of its true meaning. The words wanting in the Hebrew text, but supplied for the sake of perspicuity and precision in English, are enclosed in brackets. The slightest comparison of this with the common English translation, will show how false and absurd the latter must be. Thus the two Hebrew words *evedh* and *amau*, falsely translated "bond men" and "bond maids" in the common translation, are both in the singular number in the Hebrew text, literally meaning "manservant" and "maid" or "maiden," in Hebrew, and as such are correctly translated "servant" and "maid" in the common translation of the 6th verse of the same chapter!! The word "*quaunah*," improperly translated "buy" in the 44th and 45th verses, ought to have been literally rendered, procure, acquire, obtain, &c., in the same passages. The Hebrew word *goim*, falsely translated "heathen" in the 44th verse, always literally means "nations," and should in whatever it occurs be thus rendered. The Hebrew word *nauhal*, rendered "possess" in my translation, which is the nearest to its literal meaning, may sometimes perhaps be correctly rendered "inherit," "redeem," &c., according to the subject matter treated of, as it is in some parts of the English Scriptures, but which do not express its true meaning in the present case, as we shall soon see. The true meaning of these words was thus perverted in the common translation, because since there were no words in the Hebrew language answering to our English word "slave," "slaveholder," "slavery," &c., King James' translators, in imitation of the Catholic priests who first forged these perversions, falsely dressed up their English version of this statute, so as to resemble the modern Christian practice of negro slavery as nearly as possible--that species of slavery having at the period of their translation, under the sanction of these and similar perversions of the Scriptures, become very extensive, respectable, and popular, in several Christian countries, especially in their tropical territories. Like the false priests and Pharisees of old, these translators, in connection with many other corruptionists of their time, and with still more now existing, thus falsified the true word of God to gratify a corrupt public sentiment, and please their principal patrons for the sake of worldly popularity.

This statute was rendered necessary in the Levitical code from the fact, that by the operation of the statutes for the original distribution of land and the institution of the Jubilee, it was impossible for foreigners settling in the Israelitish nation and for their posterity to hold any real estate except during very short periods, so that it was necessary for them and their posterity, so long as they remained in the nation, to be the servants of the native Israelites, the lineal descendants of Abraham and Shem. It was in this sense alone that the Jewish nation as such, and not the individuals composing it, were to "inherit," or rather possess these adopted foreigners and their posterity, for the purpose of free and voluntary service only. To understand this intent of the statute the better it is necessary to premise, that in many parts of the Old Testament, agreeably to a Hebrew, or rather ancient oriental idiom, where a general address is in the singular number (see Ex. xx. 2-16; Prov. i. 8; Eccle. xii. 1), each individual of a nation to whom the directions of the address are applicable, is addressed separately or singly--but where a general address is in the plural number (see Deut. iv. 1-8, 15, 16,

&c.), the whole nation is addressed as one people. This is a general rule in the Old Testament, the principal exception to it being where a nation is personified and addressed accordingly, as in Deut. xxvii. 1, 2, 4, xxxi. 20, &c.

Bearing this rule in mind, the critical reader of the statute under review will observe, that at the commencement and conclusion of the statute, the Jews were addressed *distributively*, or in the singular number, as separate individuals, while in the remainder of the statute they were addressed *collectively*, or in the plural number, as a whole nation or people.

This change of the address is a circumstance which indicates, more than any other the principal object of the statute which was to encourage the settlement of foreigners in the Jewish nation, and provide for their support, for the more effectual promotion of the true religion--for which purpose it was the most equitable and excellent naturalization act that ever existed in this world. For the same righteous purpose each native Israelite was allowed by the statute, to procure as many of these foreign servants as he chose, by contracts made with the servants themselves, or with their parents or guardians, in which sense, and by which means alone, the native Jews and their posterity, were to "inherit" or "possess" these adopted foreigners and their posterity, by circumcision and incorporation into the body of the nation, after which the latter became as much "brethren" and "children of Israel" as the lineal descendants of Abraham were; while to prevent abuses of the custom, the usual salutary caution was appended to the end of the statute, forbidding the oppression of their poor brethren by individual masters. Lev. xix. 13, xxv. 17, 43; Mal. iii. 5, &c. It is well here to inform the reader that this is the universal construction of this statute by the Jews as a people, a circumstance that could not have happened, had the intent of it been to sanction human slavery. No respectable Jew now living pretends to any such belief, because the Jews have always considered it wicked. They still retain their ancient custom of employing servants differing from them in religious belief, which seems to be a perversion of it, agreeably to which the servants were to be of the same religious faith with their masters; and also absurd, since the reason of the original custom has long since ceased.

This scriptural ancient Hebrew use of the words "buy" and "sell" will be the better understood and appreciated by comparing it with the modern use of the English word "hire," used for a similar purpose. Free servants are now customarily said to be "*themselves* hired," and to "hire out *themselves*," &c., which is not in fact literally true, though to us from habit it is so. The employer of modern free servants has in fact no property in the servants themselves, but only in their time, labor and skill, which only he really hires. In like manner ancient Hebrew masters acquired no property in their "bought" and "sold" servants, but only in their time, labor and skill-- both this ancient and modern phraseology being thus incorrectly used, merely to avoid inconvenient circumlocutions.

# CHAPTER XIII

## PRO-SLAVERY PERVERSIONS OF THE OLD TESTAMENT.
### (*Continued.*)

## Examination of Deut. xx. 10-20 Josh. ix. 22, 23, 27; 1 Kings ix. 21, 26; Kings iv. 1, &c.; Neh. v. 5-13; Jer. xxxiv. 8-17.

IN Deut. xx. 10-20, is the statute regulating the treatment and disposal of those Canaanites, who should voluntarily submit to the Israelites about to invade their territory, as they are bound to agreeably to the promise of God to Abraham, which promise they doubtless well knew. According to the statute those who peaceably submitted were not to be exterminated, or banished, or in any respect enslaved, but were to become tributary to the Jews, just as the Egyptians who sold themselves to Joseph to be Pharaoh's servants, merely became tributary to the latter-- while those who should refuse to submit and dared to resist contrary to the divine command, were with one exception to be exterminated, or destroyed. In Josh. ix. 22, 23, 27, and 1 Kings ix. 21, 26, are recorded two cases of the practical application of this statute under peculiar circumstances. There is not the slightest evidence now existing to prove that this statute was ever intended or used to promote the practice of human slavery. The objects of the statutes were, not only to give the Jews the country promised to them, but also, either to reform or else to destroy the aboriginal inhabitants, neither of which could have been effected had they been reduced to slavery--for in that case it would have been just as impossible to have allowed to them the rights and privileges secured by the Levitical law, without which they could not have been reformed, as it is to our slaves now, and if they were allowed to live among the Jews, without reformation even as slaves, they would soon corrupt the whole nation. For these reasons the statute provided, either for their entire submission, or for their entire destruction--and it was only when the statute was disregarded, that they corrupted the people, and seduced them into their own destructive sins, see Judg. ii. 10-23, iii. 5, 7, 12-14. Besides, the individuals composing nations rendered merely tributary to others, are never held as property or slaves, the whole nation rather than its inhabitants being subjected. And thus even the Hebrews, though persecuted through "hard bondage" by the Egyptians, Ex. i. 14, ii. 23, &c.,

were in no respect held as property or slaves, as the whole history of their persecution clearly proves.

In 2 Kings iv. 1, Neh. v. 5-13, and Jer. xxxiv. 8-17, are several cases of severe prophetic denunciations and reproofs for violations of the Levitical statutes regulating free and voluntary service, which have just been reviewed. These cases illustrate the extreme facility with which the rich and powerful are prone to oppress the poor and helpless. But they also answer the important purpose of proving, that these political statutes must have been free or intended to regulate free service only, for had they been intended to regulate slave service or slavery, their violations never would have been complained of in the Scriptures, because such violations, according to the complaints made in the passages themselves, had the strongest tendency to promote and strengthen slavish oppression, and God is repeatedly declared in the Scriptures never to do anything in vain, see Ps. cxi. 7; Isa. xlv. 18, li. 6, Iv. 11; Jer. xxxi. 35, 36; Eze. vi. 10; Matt. x. 20, xxiv. 35; Luke xii. 36; Rom. ii. 2, iv. 16; 2 Tim. ii. 19, &c. He would never, therefore, have enacted laws for any purpose whatever, and at the same time condemn and forbid the use of the very means best adapted to promote and secure that purpose, for human slavery cannot be supported without worse oppression than is complained of in these passages. This single circumstance is an irrefutable objection to the pretended slavish nature of the ancient Hebrew servitudes. The whole history of the ancient Jewish nation, both sacred and profane, is interspersed with their violations of the Levitical code of laws, and especially of the statutes for the regulation of free service among the rest similar to those contained in the passages under consideration. On account of which same violations without repentance and reformation, the Jewish nation was, by the long threatened judgments of God, at last overthrown and destroyed.

Among these violations as they are recorded in the Scriptures, the sin of human oppression stands out the most conspicuous, as the numerous passages I have already quoted go far to prove. Yet multitudes of pro-slavery Christians at the present time contend, that these same oppressive violations, which overthrew and destroyed ancient Israel, are strong evidence that God sanctions the most oppressive practice in the world!!!

It is to be remembered in this connection that the cases now under review are those of strong censure for violations of the Levitical statutes, and not of approbation for obedience to them. With persons who are in the habit of quoting violations of laws, as evidence by analogy and not by contrast of what the laws themselves are, such reasoning may pass for sound logic, the same as that which quotes the bondage of the Jews in Egypt so severely condemned in the Scriptures, in justification of every other kind of oppression, and the massacre of infants by Pharaoh and Herod, in justification of all other massacres, or in other words to quote the divine condemnation of sins, in moral justification of the sins condemned!! It is in fact quoting one of two moral opposites, to show by analogy and not by contrast, what the other is. What would be thought of an advocate who would in a court of justice quote legal convictions of murder and other crimes condemned in a code of laws as evidence that those crimes were legalized and sanctioned by the same code? Yet there are thousands of minds in the United States sufficiently perverted and corrupted by slavery, thus to attempt the moral justification of that great crime--for as the latter is founded on perversions and other sins, so it perverts all minds within the sphere of its vicious influence--one perversion, like any other sin, being sure to produce effects similar to itself. The specific violations or sins complained of and threatened in the passages quoted from Nehemiah and Jeremiah were the neglect and refusal of the wealthy Jews to allow to their servants the full privileges of the year of Release, the Jubilee, and the redemptions by which the latter were discharged from service--in consequence of which violations, these servants were not only oppressed at home, but were sometimes obliged to sell themselves to the inhabitants of the neighboring nations, who had no such institutions, and allowed their servants no such privileges, as the whole account in the passages clearly proves.

The Jews having been at this time just delivered from a long captivity, had lost much of their knowledge and respect for the Levitical law, for which reason these and other Prophets were sent to re-convert them to its obedience. It is proper also here to remark, that the Hebrew word falsely rendered "bond-men," in the common translation of 2 Kings iv. 1, is the plural number of the word "*evedh*," and thus literally means "menservants," or "servants." So in every instance where "bond-man" and "bond woman" occur in that translation, as in

Gen. xxi. 10, 12, 13, and other passages, they are translated from "*evedh*" and "*amau*," the same literally meaning "man servant" or "servant," and "maid servant" or "maiden," being thus literally and properly translated in several other passages, as in Ex. xx. 10; Lev. xxv. 6; Neh. v. 5, &c. *As there were no Hebrew words for "slave," "slaves," &c.*, when King James' translators found passages which they thought bore the strongest resemblance to the then popular practice of negro slavery, they selected the English words that came nearest to the latter meaning, without any regard to the literal import of the words in the Hebrew text, or the real doctrine intended to be inculcated by the latter. The foregoing are all the passages in the Old Testament worthy of special notice in this connection, that have been perverted for the moral justification of human slavery. These wicked perversions were forged about four hundred and fifty years ago, to justify negro slavery, which had then lately commenced among Christians; the same perversions having previous to that time been entirely unknown, at least unknown among Christians, who had long before entirely renounced human slavery. After they had first been forged by the Catholics, Protestant theologians copied and adopted them as so much sound Christian doctrine, and that apparently without any critical examination or other care. Protestants who were so sharp as to detect those Catholic perversions which justified their own persecutions, were perfectly blind to the nature of those perversions which were intended to justify the persecution of negroes and other heathen. These perversions having been thus introduced and recommended, all the modern writers on the Hebrew servitudes have until very recently concurred in their pretended belief of the slavish nature of those servitudes, they having merely copied from each other without apparent examination or care. Abundance of this kind of concurrent human testimony can be found in favor of the moral righteousness of negro and other heathen slavery, and which many American Christians are fond of quoting for that purpose. But as this is after all nothing but human testimony made up of human opinions, so I trust the whole of it has now been shown to be erroneous and false. So well settled, and so popular indeed had the pro-slavery doctrines derived from them become, that Mr. Crothers seems to have been the first Christian writer in the world who dared, in 1833, to call the whole of these absurd perversions in question. He was soon succeeded by Mr. Dickey. And the latter by Mr. Wield, and other anti-slavery writers so that the theological credit of these wicked perversions is now extensively shaken.

# CHAPTER XIV.

## TWELVE CIRCUMSTANTIAL FACTS.

HAVING thus directly proven from the texts of the Old Testament, usually perverted for the justification of human slavery, that none of them did in the least degree sanction such slavery, but on the contrary regulated free and voluntary service only, I proceed next to produce *twelve special facts*, or doctrines contained in the Scriptures and the Law of Nature, as circumstantial evidence to prove the utter impossibility of the ancient Patriarchal and Hebrew servitudes being slavish, or in any other way oppressive. My readers will please to remember the fact, that the advocates of the pretended slavery sanctioned by the Old Testament, always refuse to quote any other part of the Scriptures in relation to the subject, except the few isolated passages which they contend justify slavery, thus entirely neglecting to examine the spirit of the Scriptures in relation to it--contrary to the universal rule of ethical construction, so to construe each part of every code of laws, that will admit of it, as to correspond with the general spirit and intent of the other parts, and thus promote the harmony of the whole code, by fulfilling the whole intent of the legislators who enacted it. The facts here alluded to are as follows:

I. The first and strongest of all these facts is, *that* THIS *pretence of Old Testament slavery has no true natural analogy to support it*--a fact of immense interest to those who believe that the Laws of Nature and Revelation exactly harmonize. The ancient "bought" and "sold" Hebrew servants certainly "sold themselves," and there is no tradition or other history in the world, of the *voluntary sales* of people to be property or slaves. It is impossible there should have been, for human slavery is just as hostile and abhorrent to the Law of Nature as any other crime of which man can be guilty, the same practice requiring the aid of other crimes for its support. For this reason human slavery is a state or condition of war, as much so as piracy or common robbery on the largest scale are--so that its victims, like those of murder, &c., have always been compelled by criminal force and violence alone to submit to it, the same as are employed to perpetrate murder, robbery, &c., against the persons of men. It is therefore just as unreasonable and absurd to suppose, that the ancient Hebrew servants customarily and voluntarily placed themselves and their families in this unhappy and helpless condition, even in pursuance of statute law, as it is to suppose that they, or anybody else, ever customarily and voluntarily submitted to be murdered or robbed, or otherwise victimized by crime. Only think of God regulating a common custom by statute law, to the very existence of which torture and murder are necessary incidents!! Besides, human slavery never could have commenced in ancient Israel or anywhere else, or even been supported afterwards, without a direct and flagrant violation of the Levitical Law against man-stealing, as well as against the oppression of the poor and helpless. So much for the probability of the pretended ancient customary Hebrew slavery.

II. The next most important of these facts is, the extreme moral violence of the Scriptures against the great sin of human oppression, including of course the most oppressive practice in the world. There is not another book extant half so condemnatory and denunciatory of this terrible sin, as the Scriptures, as a thousand extracts from all parts of them will testify. See Gen. vi. 11; Ex. iii. 9, xii. 29, xiv. 28; Job xx. 19, xxvii. 13, 23; Prov. i. 11; Isa. i. 15-24, x. 1-4, xiv. 2, xvi. 4, xix. 20, lviii. 6, 7; Eze. vii. 23, 27, ix. 9, xviii. 10-13, xxii. 29,

31; Amos iv. 1, viii. 4-8; Zeph. iii. 1-8; Zech. vii. 9, 14; Matt. xxiii. 14; James v. 4.

From the prophetic and historical portions of the Scriptures we learn that more ancient nations were threatened and destroyed, for the commission of this sin, than for that of any other,--a most ominous warning to our own nation. Now, as such is the spirit or general and collective meaning of the whole Scriptures, and as God never does anything in vain, he certainly never intended any part of the letter of his Word to contradict its spirit, by establishing and sanctioning the most oppressive practice in the world, in the very Scriptures in which he had utterly condemned and forbidden every form and degree of oppression. I will merely add, in confirmation of the doctrine, that the Scriptures have been given entirely in vain for any purpose voluntarily good, if any part of them was intended to sanction human slavery, because the latter is the moral opposite and antagonist of everything that is naturally good. But besides this general spirit of the Scriptures, several special statutes were enacted in the Levitical code, to prohibit the oppression of foreigners and strangers, such as in Ex. xxii. 21; Lev. xix. 33, 34, xxv. 35; Deut. i. 16, x. 18, 19, xxiv. 14, 15, 17,

&c., where the Israelites were forbidden under the heaviest penalties to "*vex or oppress strangers,*" and are also commanded to love, respect, and protect them. As Mr. Rankin has well remarked, "nothing could be a more direct violation of these statutes, than the practice of such slavery as exists in our slaveholding states, for nothing could more 'vex,' or 'oppress' a stranger than such bondage By these statutes, to defraud a stranger of a single day's wages is set down as a grievous crime, but how much more grievous and intolerable is the sin of taking from him both his liberty and labor for life!" Certainly if the ancient Israelites had a right to the practice of human slavery, they had a right to "vex and oppress" strangers as much as they pleased; though as they had just been delivered from the most oppressive bondage themselves, their own experience of such oppression is alleged in the Levitical law as the strongest reason why they should refrain from oppressing others, especially strangers. It does certainly seem as if those who believed the Almighty enacted such conflicting and contradictory statutes in the same code, must be a portion of the characters represented in the Scriptures as having been "given up to believe a lie." We also learn from the Levitical law (Deut. vii. 26, xiii. 17, xxiii. 18; Josh.

vi. 18, vii. 11, &c.) that no abomination or cursed thing was to be brought into the Lord's house, or to be otherwise tolerated in Israel, and we learn from the spirit of such passages as Isa. xxxiii. 15, and Jer. vii. 11, &c., that the gains of oppression were considered such. Christ drove the money changers out of the temple (Matt. xxi. 12 13, &c.) for the violation of these statutes, expressly calling them "thieves" for that reason. A code containing such a provision as this, could never have been intended to authorize such wicked gains as are obtained from a practice more oppressive than any kind of robbery, or any other known form of human oppression.

III. The next of these important facts is, the existence of the numerous important legal rights and privileges expressly vested in all classes of the ancient Hebrew servants equally, by the letter of the Levitical law and other parts of the Old Testament--it being always to be remembered that according to the laws and customs of slavery, slaves have no legal rights and privileges whatever, any more than beasts and other lawful subjects of property have. Thus, all classes of the ancient Hebrew servants were circumcised the same as children; Gen. xvii. 13, 23, 27; Ex. xii. 44, 48.

Those servants had the right of covenant with God;
Deut. xxix. 10, 11, 13. They had a right to the
passover and other feasts; Ex. xii. 44, 48, 49, xxiii.
12; Lev. xxii. 11, xxv. 1, 6, 8, 35. They enjoyed the
Sabbath and its privileges; Ex. xx. 10; Lev. xxv. 6.
They had liberal wages and good treatment; Lev.
xix. 13, xxv. 35-41; Deut. xv. 13, 14, xxiv. 14, 15;
Jer. xxii. 13, xxxiv. 14, 17, &c. They were
instructed or educated; Gen. xviii. 19; Josh. viii.
33, 35. They had a right to hold property and have
servants of their own; Lev. xxv. 49; 2 Sam. xvi. 4;
*They were governed by equal laws;* Ex. xii. 49;
Deut. xvi. 18, 19; Josh viii. 33, 35; 2 Kings xxiii. 2;
2 Chron. xxxiv. 30. They might be heirs to their
masters; Gen. xv. 3; Prov. xvii. 2. They exercised
the highest offices; Gen. xv. 2, xxiv. 2; Prov. xvii.
2. They might be soldiers; Gen. xiv. 14. If their
masters abused them to the extent of mayhem, they
were set free; Ex. xxi. 26, 27. They might contend
with their masters; Job xxxi. 13. They might leave
their masters for ill-usage, of which they were to be
the sole judges; Deut. xxiii. 15, 16. They enjoyed
the great civil right of periodical freedom or
discharge from service by contract, either at the
year of release or at the Jubilee, or at both; Ex. xxi.
2; Lev. xxv. 10; Deut. xv. 12; Neh. v. 11; Jer.
xxxiv. 14. 17. They married into their masters'

families Ex. xxi. 8, 9; 1 Chron. ii. 34, 35. They were treated with respect; 1 Sam. ix. 22. The children and heirs of masters seem to have no more nor greater privileges than these servants had; see Gal. iv. 1. Now as the legal enjoyment of any one of these rights and privileges will destroy slavery, how could it have existed in a nation where they were all allowed and enjoyed? And what right have we to believe that the Almighty ever established an institution in a code of laws which he had provided the surest means of subverting and destroying in the same code? It is undoubtedly highly absurd to imagine God capable of such absurdity.

Mr. Weld in his Bible argument described several of these important rights and their effects at length, and has clearly proven, first, that they were common to every class of Hebrew servants, and secondly, that slavery could not have existed in the Jewish nation with their full exercise; see Ex. xii. 48, 49; Numb. ix. 14, xv. 15, 16, 29, &c.

IV. Another of these decisive facts is the entire absence of any slave code, or body of slave regulations, in the Levitical law, or in any other part of the Old Testament, but on the contrary, as we have seen, the direct reverse of them in all respects. This omission and antagonism are unaccountable on the hypothesis of ancient Hebrew slavery, because every nation, ancient or modern, which has ever practiced human slavery, has necessarily adopted two distinct codes of laws, one for its free inhabitants, and the other for its slaves,--the latter being in all respects exceedingly barbarous and cruel, because slavery cannot be supported at all, without the assistance of the most barbarous cruelty. Each of our slave states has now such a code, in the fabrication and support of which our slaves had no more agency than so many cattle and horses. According to Stroud and other writers on the subject of these laws, by virtue of these slave codes in this enlightened republican country, more than seventy acts punishable with death when committed by slaves, are either not punishable at all, or else in a very light or mild degree when committed by freemen,--so that the torture and murder of slaves is legalized in the slave States. Yet the whole of this barbarous and criminal legislation is indispensable to the support of slavery, because crime can only be supported by crime.

Now, as there is no trace of any such code in the Levitical law, or any other part of the old

Testament, but on the contrary, as all the Israelites were governed by one code only (Ex. xii. 49; Deut. xvi. 18, 19; Josh. viii. 33, 35, &c.), the omission can only be accounted for on the supposition that human slavery was in no respect sanctioned by the Levitical law, and did not exist in the ancient Hebrew nation at all. Had God authorized slavery by that law, he would certainly have enacted a slave code to support it, as indispensable means for that support, and the fact that he did not is sufficient evidence of itself alone, where there is no other, that he did not establish such an institution in ancient Israel. Nor is there any history of slavish or other oppression in that nation, either ancient or modern, except by the violation and not by the observance of the Levitical law, together with the consequent divine punishments of such violations. That great code was the most perfectly framed and adapted to prevent every species and degree of human oppression, of any that men were governed by, see Ex. xxii. 25, 27; Lev. xix. 9, 10, 15, xxiii. 22; Deut. i. 17, xv. 7-15, xvi. 19, xxiv. 6, 10, 13, 19-22, xxvii. 19, &c. The spirit of these and the numerous similar provisions found in the Scriptures, ought to be infused into all the human legislation in the world.

V. Another important and decisive fact is, that, as has been already remarked, there are no words in the Hebrew language corresponding in meaning with our English, and the ancient and modern words "slave," "slaveholder," "slavery," &c., a circumstance which never could have happened had the practice of human slavery existed among the ancient Israelites, either with or without the Levitical law. Never did an important public institution, custom, or practice, exist in any country in the world, without a distinct and specific name given to it in the language of the country. Accordingly the ancient Greeks and Romans, and other ancient nations, as well as the modern English, French, Spaniards, &c., who have adopted and pursued the practice of human slavery, have each specific words or names for the practice itself, and for those who pursue it, and for their victims in the practice, in their respective languages.

This fact alone is of itself sufficient also to prove that human slavery never could have existed among the ancient Hebrews. I do not know that God ever expressly created language in the  world, but I do know that He created men with faculties and a disposition to give specific names to every important thing in the world, they were specially interested in or affected by, as the structure of every language in the world will testify.[*]

*There is no word in the Hebrew language that means any such thing as our word slave. The Hebrew word which is in the king's translation rendered both servant and bond servant, is Gnabad; the a is pronounced long in both syllables. The word is used five times in the Old Testament as a proper name, once by itself, in the case of the grandfather of David the King, where it is in our translation Obed--the nasal gn being left off, following the Greek version of the Septuagint, and not the Hebrew. In four other instances it is used where it is compounded with other words--(gnabad Edom, the servant of Edom), OBADIAH (gnabad Yahovauzh, the servant of Jehovah), ABEDNEGO (gnabad nago, the servant of light), EBEDMELIK (gnabad malak, the servant of the King).*

The root of this word is the verb GNANBAD (in the last syllable the a is short as in sad), which is thus defined by the highest Hebrew authorities-- to Labor--to cultivate--to labor for, or serve any one--to be tributary. But if the word signifies a slave, then was father Adam in the garden of Eden a slave; for God saw that "there was not a man to till" or cultivate the ground, and for this purpose he made man; and the aforesaid word is the identical word there rendered " to till," or cultivate.

VI. Another of these important facts is, the Levitical statute for the voluntary escape of the ancient Hebrew servants from their masters, contained in Deut. xxiii. 15, 16. Under this important statute the servant could leave his master's service whenever he pleased, and could not be compelled to return to that service without his own free consent; he himself being, in every case, the sole judge of the justice and propriety of the whole transaction, the statute being thus the direct moral and political opposite of our laws for the arrest and return of innocent fugitive slaves. This humane statute is the spirit of the whole Scriptures, and those violate that spirit who forcibly seize and return innocent fugitives from slavish oppression or who do not shield and protect them, see Prov. xxxi. 8, 9; Isa. i. 17, xvi. 3, 4, lviii. 7; Jer. xxi. 12, xxii. 3; Eze. xviii. 7; Oba. 10-15; Zech. vii. 9-14; Matt. xxv. 35, &c. Some contend that this statute was for the relief of foreign fugitive servants or slaves only, but the generality of the language of the statute proves, that it was intended for the benefit of all servants alike, domestic as well as foreign. It is, however, a provision most effectually adapted to guard and protect the rights and happiness of servants that ever was devised in the world, the same being rendered necessary for that special purpose, by the uncommon liability of that class of persons to civil oppression, and will of itself alone, wherever it is adopted in legal practice, put an end to the practice of human slavery, in a week,--a circumstance which leads us to marvel why, if God really intended to establish such slavery by the Levitical law, He should insert a provision in the same code, which could not fail to prevent the commencement of the practice. It is truly wicked to imagine God capable of such folly, see Job iv. 17, 19, xl. 2, &c. Yet strange and horrible to relate, this very conduct in oppressed slaves, thus approbated and sanctioned by the law of God, is in an enlightened country, and among a people professing to believe in the Christian religion, considered as one of the most heinous crimes that slaves can commit, and such as to render them deserving of the severest slave punishment!! And those freemen who have acted in accordance with the dictates of humanity and the Laws of God, and relieved those fugitives from slavery, have been, and some of them are now, suffering the penalty within the walls of the prisons of our Slave States. One man, like Gen. Lafayette, is extolled to the skies, and triumphal arches are erected throughout our land in his honor, because he left his country and volunteered to aid us in obtaining our political rights and liberties while another is made to pass, not under an arch of triumphal wreaths, but under the arch of a prison door, to remain many years, because he aided his fellow mortals in obtaining, not their political, but their personal liberty. "Oh, my country, where is thy consistency?"

Such conduct reminds us of the persecution of Christians by the heathen, for their obedience to the Law of God.

VII. Another fact of immense importance in this connection is, the great Levitical institutions of the year of Release and the Jubilee, see Ex. xxi. 2; Lev. xxv. 8, 13; Deut. xv. 12, &c. These were both types of deliverance from spiritual bondage, but another great use was found in their civil policy. Out of the abundant caution in favor of the rights of men, these institutions were intended to prevent contracts for service extending beyond certain periods, and for the discharge of servants, not from slavery, which did not exist in the Hebrew nation, but from their own voluntary contracts for service (if indeed they could contract beyond those periods), which might otherwise be most oppressively extended beyond them. These institutions being thus established to protect civil liberty, could never have been extended to sanction human slavery - nor would God ever have enacted them, had He intended any such sanction; because, so long as they remained in force, it was impossible for slavery to exist. By the operation of the Jubilee more was done to prevent the oppression of the poor, than by all the human laws for that purpose ever enacted in the world. Any law enacted to protect natural liberty and rights, can never, while it is faithfully obeyed, be made to protect its moral opposites.

VIII. Another highly important fact resulting from the Jubilee is the restoration of Inheritances or Estates to the original owners or their heirs, on the arrival of each successive Jubilee, see Lev. xxv. 10, 13, 23, 24, 25, 31, 41 ; Num. xxxvi. 4, &c. This provision was intended for the especial benefit of the poor, particularly for the benefit of poor Hebrew servants, without any regard to the pecuniary interest of their former masters. At the conquest of the Land of Canaan, all the conquered territory was as equally divided among the Israelitish people as possible, see Num. xxvi. 52. 56, xxxiii. 54; Josh. xi. 23, xiv. 1, 5, &c., which division was by the institution of the Jubilee, like our policy or system of entailment, rendered perpetual to the posterity of the original owners.

The conduct of those who quote the perverted passages which have been reviewed in favor of slavery, is certainly very remarkable - for they utterly refuse to allow any other part of the Levitical law to regulate the condition of modern slaves, contrary to the well known legal rule which teaches, that all parts of the same code in relation to the same subject matter, ought in justice and according to custom in other cases, to be adopted and applied to its regulation, or else reject all. Thus they will allow of no statute for the voluntary escape of slaves, no year of Release, no Jubilee, no Restoration of property, no wages or other pay, nor any of the other Levitical rights and privileges to slaves, merely because such an allowance would spoil their whole theological slave-theory, and instantly destroy that beautiful system of Scriptural slave bondage and oppression, which they pretend God himself established by those perverted statutes. It seems to me that they must have but little confidence in the wisdom of their Maker, thus to adopt only a small portion of His pretended law on the subject of slavery, and reject all the rest of it appertaining to the same subject.

IX. Another most decisive fact is, that there is not only no account in the Scriptures of any kind of Slavery in the Jewish nation, but there is no Jewish or other tradition of any such slavery. Every other ancient slaveholding nation has left distinct historical traditions of its slaveholding practice--it being just as impossible for a nation to forget the principal occurrences in its own history, as it is for an individual to forget those of his own life. If ever, therefore, the Jews had practiced human slavery, even in violation of the Levitical law, they would have left an historical tradition of it, the same as the Greeks and Romans have of their history--while the entire absence of any such history is the strongest negative testimony that can exist, that the Jews never had any such practice or custom among them. Josephus relates no such custom, though the word "slave" is made to appear in the English translation of his history, which is most likely to be a false rendering, because the Hebrew language, which contains no such word, was his native tongue. That the Jews were sometimes guilty of great oppression and other sins against the Levitical law, is certain from the Scriptures themselves, see Isa. i. 11-15, xxix. 13; Jer. xxii. 13-17; Matt. xv. 6, 9; Mark vii. 5, 9; Tit. i. 14, &c. It appears to have been chiefly on account of this very sin that most of the Prophets were commissioned and sent to reprove them. But there is no evidence whatever that they carried these abominable perversions to the extent our modern Christians have, to the moral justification of actual slavery or property in man.

X. Another fact is, that at the creation God gave to mankind alone, the dominion of ownership or property in the earth and its productions, see Gen. i. 26, 28, ix. 2; Ps. viii. 6, 8, &c. By virtue of this great statutory grant, one individual of the human race has just as good natural and divine right to the earth and its productions, as any other individual has, of which right every kind of monopoly is a direct infringement and breach of the moral law of God, and to the full and perfect enjoyment of which grant and right, it is necessary that each individual should be just as free as all the rest are. This statute strikes at the root of not only slavery, but of monopoly; by rendering each a violation of the moral law. Thus does the first chapter in the Scriptures contain, by an implied but necessary divine guaranty, the grand charter of the civil liberties of all mankind--a charter violated by slaveholders, and other monopolists, and by oppressors every moment of their oppressive agency. God himself has thus forbidden all human monopoly by His own holy and perfect law. He never made a grant to one class of men of any other class, and the fact that he has not, taken in connection with the other grant, is alone proof certain and conclusive, that so far from ever having sanctioned the practice of human slavery, He utterly forbade the same by enactments, obedience to which rendered such slavery impossible.

XI. Another equally decisive fact is, that human slavery is a direct violation of the eighth and tenth commandments, and an indirect but equally certain violation of the other commands contained in that great table. Slavery, as we have seen, is the highest kind of larceny condemned by the Levitical law, and is therefore the greatest possible violation of the eighth commandment. But as by the same law every human being is, under God, the sole owner of himself and all his just rights, faculties and acquisitions, the crime which usurps and robs him of them all is founded in covetousness, or in a greedy and criminal desire to possess that which belongs to another, or to others, and to which the slaveholder knows he has no moral or just right, and which is thus a direct violation of the tenth commandment. But human slavery is also an indirect but equally certain violation of the commands in the Decalogue, because its support and effects necessarily produce such violations, as every reader will by a little reflection readily perceive. Now nothing could be more wickedly absurd than the supposition, that though the Almighty enacted these great commands in the Levitical law, He at the same time established an institution in the same law, the support of which He knew would produce the necessary and certain violation of the same commands, and within the wide sphere of its destructive influence, render the practical observance and operation of the whole of them impossible.

Slavery produces the constant violation of the commands of the Decalogue. Thus, it compels the slaves to violate the first and second commands, by rendering their masters the objects of their slavish obedience and worship, and compelling them to obey their owners' will in every case, though that will be ever so hostile to that of God. It produces the violation of the third command, by the constant criminal temptation and wicked necessity in all concerned in, or suffering from it, to use the most profane language, and causes them otherwise lightly to treat their Maker's commands. It teaches them also to violate the fourth command, by rendering it impossible for slaves to observe the Lord's day (the Christian's Sabbath), in the spirit of the command, and by otherwise inducing a general neglect and disregard in all slave societies to the ordinances to be attended to on that day; of the fifth, by prohibiting slave children from honoring and obeying their own parents, they being obliged to substitute in place of filial obedience and parental authority, a slavish obedience and subjection to their masters only; of the sixth, by constantly tempting and producing slave murders in every form and degree of barbarity, for the necessary support of slavery; of the seventh, by prohibiting marriage to the slaves, and producing criminal concubinage and licentiousness among them, as well as the general compulsory prostitution of the female portion of the slaves, by reason of the arbitrary power which it confers on the masters and other oppressors; and lastly, of the ninth, by its necessary tendency to produce the habit of falsehood and lying in both masters and slaves--in the former for the purpose of deceiving and abusing their slaves, in the latter to deceive their oppressors and avoid punishment for slave offences. It also produces the same habit in others who are infected with the spirit of the sin of slavery and are enlisted in its support, as is well exemplified by their constant employment of the various false pretences and objections raised by them against the abolition of slavery, and by the malignant falsehoods circulated by them against the friends of emancipation, and their measures, as well as against and respecting slaves; and as all the other moral precepts in the Scriptures are but exemplifications and applications of those in the Decalogue, slavery directly or indirectly produces the constant necessary violation of them all.

XII. The last decisive fact I shall quote in this connection is, that human slavery is an indirect but certain violation of every moral precept contained in the Scriptures, because the support of it produces the necessary violation of every one of those precepts, a circumstance which proves its great criminality, and furnishes the principal reason why it was punished with death by the Levitical law. In this way such slavery is discovered to violate the spirit or general intent of the Scriptures more extensively perhaps than any other crime except murder. It is impossible for any person to practice human slavery an hour without violating the law of Love, the Golden Rule, and the numerous other similar precepts that abound in the Scriptures, as much so as if he practiced murder and other crimes, as every one would acknowledge were he himself enslaved, and as the slightest critical reflection will demonstrate. Thus it is impossible for any slaveholder or other person engaged in the support of slavery not to violate the precepts found in such passages as Lev. xix. 13; Deut. xxiv. 14, 15; Mal. iii. 5; Mark x. 19; 1 Thes. iv. 6, &c. Nor is it possible for any slave fully to obey the precepts in Ex. xx. 16; Eph. v. 2-4, 22, 25, vi. 1, 4. Now for us to pretend that the Almighty would give us this multitude of precepts as rules of our moral conduct, and declare disobedience to any of them to be sinful, and at the same time establish and sanction an institution in the same law containing the precepts, the necessary effect of which he foreknew would produce the necessary violation of them all, and totally prevent their moral efficacy in this world, is an absurdity too gross and too wicked for a moment's innocent toleration.

I might thus proceed to enumerate many other natural and Scriptural facts of less moral importance in the connection, but equally conclusive against the wicked pretence of Old Testament slavery, but the foregoing are abundantly sufficient for the present purpose. And against this overwhelming mass of circumstantial evidence, contradicting and disproving the pretence, what do its advocates produce? Nothing but a repetition of the few perverted passages which have been reviewed, their pro-slavery construction of which has been proved to be false, as the same passages were intended for the promotion of liberty instead of slavery--the same repetition being always accompanied with a contemptuous and obstinate refusal, either critically to examine the merits of those passages by themselves, or to compare the passages with the context on the same subject matters, or with the general spirit of the Scriptures, in order to ascertain their true and genuine meaning. Such dishonesty as this is truly popish in its character, and never was, and never can be employed for anything but the justification of sin and crime, being always exhibited in cases where the true meaning of God's Word is the subject of controversy, the same conduct being a direct violation of the precepts contained in 1 Thes. v. 21, and other similar passages, and severely censured and condemned in Matt. xv. 3, 6, 9; 2 Pet. ii. 1, and in a hundred other places, and can only be accounted for in the present case, from the absolute necessity of committing one great crime for the support of another, because sin can never in any case or under any circumstances be supported by any other than sinful means.

# CHAPTER XV.

## PRO-SLAVERY PERVERSIONS OF THE NEW TESTAMENT.
## INTRODUCTORY REMARKS.

IT is very generally contended by the advocates of human slavery that Christ and his apostles did not condemn the practice of such slavery, but, on the contrary, connived at, and acquiesced in, and thereby sanctioned that practice, though the same was nearly universal throughout the Roman empire during the whole period of their ministry. This pretended example of theirs is supposed to be a sufficient moral warrant for the pro-slavery conduct and example of our pro-slavery clergy and their pro-slavery followers. It is said if Christ and his true followers sanctioned and supported human slavery, all Christians ought to sanction and support the practice also. But to this pro-slavery pretence, I reply, that Christ DID DIRECTLY AND EXPRESSLY CONDEMN THE PRACTICE OF HUMAN SLAVERY AS A GREAT SIN, and by the same name of man stealing, &c., too; in the same manner as the Old Testament did, as has been sufficiently explained. He did this by solemnly re-affirming, ratifying, and confirming the Levitical or Moral law, which said law condemned human slavery by those names, as we have seen it did; see Matt. v. 17, 18; Luke xvi. 17. Were a legislature to adopt and ratify a whole code of laws at once, as has been the case, which said code condemned a particular act or practice as a crime or sin, it would just as directly and as positively condemn the same act or practice as a crime or sin, as if it had originally draughted and enacted the special statute intended for that purpose. It is the weakest sophistry imaginable to pretend that Christ did not condemn human slavery directly, because he could not ratify and confirm the moral law without doing so. It would be just as absurd and false to pretend that Christ did not by such ratification and confirmation directly condemn murder, robbery, theft, and the other crimes specifically condemned in the moral law or Levitical code, as that he did not directly condemn manstealing or slavery by it. The apostles also pronounced the same condemnation by their similar ratification and confirmation of the moral law. See Rom. iii. 31, vii. 12, x. 4; Gal. iii. 24; 1st Tim. i. 8, and numerous other New Testament passages confirmatory of the moral law. The whole public ministry of the apostles was based upon this doctrine, namely,--that the whole moral law was still in force, and would for ever remain in force; and that as all mankind had violated that law, and would continue to violate it, they had no other means of salvation left but by faith in Christ and obedience to His laws. The whole scope and tenor of their writings so clearly and abundantly teach this doctrine that it cannot be honestly mistaken. After such repeated and explicit ratifications and confirmations of this great law, there was neither any necessity nor propriety in Christ and the apostles transcribing the whole of that law into their writings in order to show that they condemned each of the specific crimes enumerated in it, such a transcript being a work of mere supererogation or useless task. Accordingly they never alluded to any of the specific sins condemned in and by the moral law for any other purpose than that of illustration, as in 1st Tim i. 10, and other passages. But even without such allusions, the mere ratification and confirmation of the moral law by Christ and his apostles, was a direct and positive condemnation by them of every sin condemned in that law. The common pro-slavery pretence, therefore, that Christ and his apostles did not condemn human slavery, is a naked and obvious untruth. They did in various other ways indirectly condemn such slavery, as by their denunciations of oppression, and their views of covetousness, extortion, &c., but the foregoing is their direct and positive condemnation.

So by way of indirect apology, we frequently hear it asserted that Christ and his apostles did not attack slavery at all, that they never preached against it, and from this assumption the pro-slavery inference is sagaciously drawn that they actually connived at and acquiesced in the practice, just as pro-slavery preachers and professors now do. But to this gratuitous supposition, or begging the question, I reply, that we do not now know against what particular sins Christ and his apostles preached the most; for the New Testament is merely a general history and compilation of general doctrines, and not a volume of their religious discourses. Among the various sins, it specifically mentions murder, and manstealing or slavery, and condemns them both with equal severity, but it gives us but a small share of the preaching of Christ and his apostles, and none at all of their specific preaching against those two sins. According to this pretended negative testimony of the New Testament then, if Christ and his apostles connived at and approbated the practice of slavery, they connived at and approbated the practice of murder also. So according to the same mode of reasoning, as we have no account whatever that Christ and his apostles preached against piracy, arson, forgery, counterfeiting, &c. they must have connived at and approbated the practice of those crimes, and have thereby left us their Christian sanction to practice the same, just us we are to practice murder and slavery! Such are the necessary moral consequences of this kind of perversion.

During the public ministry of Christ and his apostles, murder and slavery, and most other crimes condemned by the moral law, abounded in the Roman empire, and I infer that they preached just as faithfully against slavery as against murder and those other crimes, because they were all persecuted, and all but one put to death, on account of their preaching, which they hardly would have been had they, like many of our modern preachers and professors of religion, connived at and acquiesced in the customary practice of those most popular sins. Faithful Christian preaching always brought persecution upon itself. Had the apostles been unfaithful or treacherous to their cause by conniving at popular sins, they might have lived quietly, peaceably, and respectably, among Roman murderers, menstealers, idolators, &c., and been patronized, cherished, and esteemed by them just as our modern pro-slavery preachers now are by American slaveholders. So far as we have any account of their preaching in the New Testament, the presumption is, that Christ and his apostles faithfully preached against every form and degree of customary sin in their times, as Matthew xxiii., Luke xi., and other specimens testify, or in other words that they preached against all the sins condemned by the moral law which they had ratified, and to this reasonable presumption there is no opposing testimony. We are nowhere positively informed in the New Testament, or elsewhere, that the Apostles, in their ordinary verbal discourses, preached against the cruel heathen persecutions of themselves and other Christians, against offensive war, theatrical exhibitions, gladiatorial shows, human sacrifices, concubinage, heathen feasts, idol worship, the Olympic games, and a hundred other heathen abominations legalized and customarily prevalent in their times. But whoever supposes that they did not preach against all these abominations, or that they in any way winked at and approbated the practice of them, must, in my opinion, be entirely mistaken, because there is no probability that they were thus treacherous to the moral law which they had ratified, and because their fate proves they were not. Nor have we any more evidence or reason to believe that Christ and his apostles connived at and approbated the practice of slavery and its horrors, than that they connived at and approbated the practice of murder or the other heathen abominations here specified. As the perversions by means of which so many of our American Christians pacify their consciences were then unknown, no satisfactory reason can now be rendered why they should or might have been liable to do so.

From some statements in the New Testament it would seem that the preaching of Christ and his Apostles must have been extensive indeed; see Matt. x. 17, xxviii. 19, 20; Luke ix. 2, 6; John xxi. 25; Acts i. 8, ix. 15, x. 42, xiii. 5, xvi. 10, xvii. 2, 17, xviii. 4, 25, xx. 20, 25-27; 1 Cor. xv. 10; 2 Cor. xi. 23, 28, &c. Thus we are informed in Acts xxviii. 30, 31, that Paul preached two years in one place at one time, yet we have scarcely any information in the New Testament, or in any other history, respecting the specific subjects of the voluminous public discourses of these great preachers. We have no specific information in the New Testament, or elsewhere, that they preached against slavery or any other criminal practice by its specific name. But as the same great Apostle has informed us, in Acts xx. 26, 27, that "he had not shunned to declare *all* the counsel of God," that "he was pure from the blood of all men," and as he, in Eph. vi. 20, 21, and other passages, requested the prayers of the brethren for special grace to preach the gospel boldly, which he could not have done without faithfully preaching against slavery or man-stealing, we may confidently conclude that he and all the other apostolic preachers did so.

There is no probability that these devoted men neglected to preach anything they taught, or that they failed to preach against any crime condemned in their writings, not even slavery. Yet we are gravely informed by our pro-slavery preachers and their followers, that we have no authority from the New Testament to preach against slavery, and thereby disturb the domestic scriptural relation of master and slave, and that we ought silently to acquiesce in, and thus sanction the relation, just as Christ and his apostles must be supposed to have done. This is the kind of gospel extensively preached in this country at this time. It will be a matter of amusement if not of profit, to test the correctness of this mode of preaching by its consequences. For instance, as nothing is said in the New Testament about any public preaching of Christ and his apostles against murder, we have no authority from the volume, according to this reasoning to preach against murder, the same being thus licensed by that book! In the same manner as nothing is said in that book about any public preaching of the apostles against arbitrary government, and despotic law, and practice, we are to infer from these negative premises that the same apostles connived at, acquiesced in, and approbated the barbarities of Nero, Caligula, Domitian, and the other heathen monsters who persecuted and murdered them and their brethren! and that this supposed connivance and assent of the apostles is to be construed as a moral justification of those barbarities, and moral license to similar atrocities in all after time! On the same kind of premises we are also required to believe that John the Baptist and Christ both approbated the massacre of the infants by Herod, and that public massacres of all sorts are to be silently tolerated by Christians! So that Protestants have no authority from the scriptures, and therefore no moral right whatever, to complain of their persecutions by the Catholics, which they ought to approbate and not condemn; nor have the persecuted a right to complain of their persecutors under any circumstances! such persecutions being morally justified and sanctioned by the approving silence of Christ and his apostles!

Furthermore, as we have no account whatever of any public preaching by Christ and his Apostles against forgery, arson, piracy counterfeiting, and twenty other heinous ancient as well as modern crimes, we are to presume from this supposed approving silence and acquiescence of theirs, that the whole of those crimes are morally approbated and licensed in the New Testament, by the special example of Christ and his Apostles, so that we have no moral right whatever to disturb others in the commission of them!! And lastly, as there is no account of any such preaching of Christ and his Apostles against human slavery, nor against the moral crimes necessary to support and preserve the practice, we are to presume that the whole of these crimes are morally approbated and licensed in the New Testament, by the approving silence and connivance of Christ and his Apostles, and were thus morally justified by the same example at all times and places thereafter!! These few test specimens are abundantly sufficient to prove the falsity, absurdity, and futility of the nonsense that we have no authority in the New Testament, from the writings of Christ and his Apostles, for preaching and inveighing against the system of human slavery that exists in our land; on the contrary, it is just as easy to prove that we have this authority from the New as we have from the Old Testament, for the latter is entirely ratified and confirmed by the former, as we have seen, and whatever any part of both, or either of them, condemn and oppose, or ratify and approve, we all are morally bound to ratify and approve, or condemn and oppose, as the case may be, and that by public preaching, as well as in all other just and righteous modes, see Rom. xv. 4; 2 Tim. iii. 16, 17, &c. Nobody doubts the truth of this great moral duty in any other case except slavery. Nor does anybody doubt in any other case, the special obligation of the Christian pulpit to practice this duty, since the Scriptures plainly teach the special obligation of that agency to enforce every Christian duty, and that with a degree of energy and perseverance proportioned to the public neglect of each duty, as is best shown by special precept and the examples of the Holy Prophets and Apostles, who literally discharged this duty. When therefore we know that both the Old and New Testament condemn and oppose slavery, with the same severity as they do the worst of other crimes, as has been clearly shown in these passages, we also know from the same Scriptures, that it is our moral duty to condemn and oppose it with equal severity ourselves.

# CHAPTER XVI.

## PRO-SLAVERY PERVERSIONS OF THE NEW TESTAMENT.
### (*Continued.*)

## Examination of Matt. xx. 28, xxvi. 28; Acts xx. 28; Rom. vii. 14; 1 Cor. vi. 20, vii. 23; 1 Pet. i. 18, 19; 2 Pet. ii. 1, 3; Rev. v. 9, &c.

IT has already been sufficiently explained, that the whole of these passages are typical or figurative descriptions of free and voluntary service, copied from their Levitical types or figures of the ancient Hebrew servitudes, and are so far from being indicative of involuntary or slavish service, that they figuratively describe a "ransom," or a "purchase," or a "redemption," each meaning substantially the same effect or thing, from the slavish service or slavery of sin, to the free and voluntary service of righteousness. Every reader of the Scriptures understands the passages in this sense without a dissenting opinion or doubt, notwithstanding the employment in the descriptions of the words "buy," "sell," "purchase" and "redeem," &c. The types or figures from which these descriptions are taken, are the same ancient

Hebrew sales, purchases, ransoms, and redemptions of the ancient Hebrew and other oriental servants, wives, children, wards, brethren, and other relations, so often mentioned in the Pentateuch and other parts of the Old Testament, as in Gen. xvii. 12, 13, &c. Ex. xxi. 2, &c., xxx. 12-16; Lev. v. 6-19, xxv. 48, 49; Num. xxxi. 50; Deut. xvi. 12, &c. Ruth iv. 10, &c. transactions frequently alluded to for the purpose of illustration in other parts of the Old Testament, see Job. xxxiii. 21, xxxvi. 18; Ps. xlix. 7, 8, &c. We know that these ancient customary transactions were the types or figures from which the New Testament passages now under review were taken, not only because no other ancient types of the kind are to be found, and because all the formative descriptions in the New Testament of free and voluntary service are copied from the Levitical types, in the Old Testament, but also from direct allusions to these types in various other parts of the New Testament, see Gal. iv. 1-5, v. 1; Heb. ix. 9, x. 1, 4, &c. No one ever thinks of doubting the truth of these figurative allusions in favor of anything else but human slavery.

But, as has been already remarked, since these New Testament descriptions are of free and voluntary service only, the types or figures from which they were taken must have been of similar free service, because a free description cannot be taken from a slavish type. It is impossible therefore that any of the Old Testament purchases and sales of human beings should have been of a slavish nature, unless, as in the case of the sale of Joseph by his brethren, the subject matter and the general description together both combine to show clearly that such was the fact. For these reasons it is perfectly clear from the whole tenor of the Scriptures, that none of the ancient Hebrew servants were any more sold into involuntary service or slavery, than Christian converts were as such ever reduced to that condition by their Christian conversion--both kinds of these servitudes being perfectly free and voluntary.

# CHAPTER XVII.

## PRO-SLAVERY PERVERSIONS OF THE NEW TESTAMENT.
### (*Continued.*)

### Examination of Matt. xviii. 23, 25, xxii. 27; Rom. xiii. 1-7; Titus iii. 1; 1 1 Pet. ii. 13.

IT is impossible that the case recorded in Matt. xviii. 23, 25, should have been a slave sale or even a figurative description of one, because it appears from the 24th verse of the same chapter that the servant spoken of "*owed*" his master, which was impossible if he were a slave, because by the laws of human slavery, both ancient and modern, a slave could no more owe his master, than a beast or other article of property could. By the law of God, by the common law, and by every other just code of laws in the world, every slaveholder justly owes his slave, and not the latter him, a doctrine from which the Abolitionists contend that compensation on emancipation is morally and justly due to the slaves alone, and to nobody else, and that from their former masters or oppressors only. The parable recorded in the passage under consideration, is an allusion to the sales of insolvent debtors under the harsh and oppressive heathen laws of the Roman Empire, the same being in no way similar to any voluntary sales of persons approved in the Old Testament, and was used in this New Testament passage to illustrate the doctrine the Saviour was then inculcating.

Both the letter and spirit of Matt. xxii. 21; Rom. xiii. 1-7; Titus iii. 1; 1 Pet. ii. 13, and similar passages, are for the sake of human slavery most grossly perverted by the advocates of such slavery, to teach a silent acquiescence in, and contented submission to the practice of all such public sins as are legalized by wicked human governments. From the doctrine promulgated in Rom. xiii. 1-7, and many corresponding passages, it is certain that human governments of every name and form are of divine appointment and authority, and are to be respected and obeyed as such. But such governments and their abuses being moral and political opposites, the doctrine gives no moral license, and imposes no moral duty whatever, to respect and support the abuses, the perversions, and the corruptions of such governments, for the administration of the latter must be morally righteous and good, to warrant the voluntary support of them as a moral duty in any case whatever, because we are directed to avoid all sin and the support of all sinful agents and agencies. Not that the Scriptures do not make a just distinction between forms of human government, because they plainly teach a preference of the republican form over all others. But they also teach, that God will own and bless any other form of government that is righteously and wisely administered, and also, that He will disown and curse any form, even the republican, that is perverted and abused to be the shield and protector of public sins--and as the same Scriptures also teach, that as far as we are capable, we are morally bound to imitate God as the first and greatest rule of moral duty, so we are morally bound to oppose all governmental abuses and corruptions whatever, without regard to modes and forms.

The whole of this Scriptural teaching exactly corresponds with the great Law of Nature, because our own common sense teaches us that one form or mode of government is no better than another, except as it is less liable to abuse. But the advocates of human slavery contend in its behalf, that we are morally bound by the instructions of the passages under consideration, voluntarily to support all the errors, abuses, perversions and corruptions of human governments, legalized human slavery among the rest, and never attempt to use even moral means to counteract and destroy, or reform it.

But this kind of sophistry must be very difficult to support by argument, for on the supposition that it is true doctrine, Christ and his Apostles and disciples were morally bound to justify and support their own persecutors, instead of blaming and condemning them as they did, because all the persecutions they suffered were legalized by human governments. This slavish doctrine must be heretical in every respect. Thus, human life and faculties, as well as human governments, are also of divine appointment and authority, and we are directed in the Scriptures to preserve and support and employ them properly, but it must be highly sinful in us to justify and support their abuses, because the latter are highly sinful.

Besides, we are directly and repeatedly taught in the Scriptures, both by precept and example, that where the laws and customs of men conflict with the law of God, we are morally bound to obey the latter, though the consequences be a necessary violation of the former, see Ex. xxiii. 2; Acts iv. 19, v. 29 , and numerous corroborative passages; a doctrine fully illustrated and confirmed by the voluntary and consistent example of all the Bible preachers, the whole of whom were persecuted and most of them put to death, for their voluntary violation of wicked human laws and customs. Nothing can be morally and politically more reasonable than this conduct, or in other words more agreeable to the Law of Nature, because, though human governments are divinely authorized, yet their abuses and corruptions are not, and are therefore entitled to no voluntary respect and support. It is remarkable that in the passages now under consideration we are commanded not to *obey* human governments and laws but to *submit* to, or be *subject* to them, and that for the Lord's sake and not theirs. If therefore we violate wicked human laws, but voluntarily and peaceably submit to their penalties inflicted for the violation, we as truly remain subject or submissive to them, as if we obeyed their requirements. From these plain premises it clearly appears, that the subjection inculcated in Rom. xiii. 1-7, &c., really means, voluntary obedience to all human laws and customs that are morally good, and voluntary submission to the penalties prescribed for the violation of all those that are morally bad, see Daniel iii. 6, &c. This reasonable construction harmonizes with the entire teaching of the Scriptures on the subject, which the opposite pro-slavery construction entirely destroys. It is a doctrine of the Scriptures too plain to be innocently misunderstood, that wherever we find the laws and customs of men conflict with the law of God, we are morally bound to violate the former in obedience to the latter. Others carry the perversion still further, and maintain that because we are morally bound peaceably to submit to these wicked penalties, at least unless we can peaceably avoid their infliction, and because we have no moral right to resist their infliction by physical force, therefore the wickedest human governments have a moral or divine right to legalize and enforce those penalties. But this pretence must also be a rank and dangerous heresy, because, if it be true doctrine, where is the moral guilt of legalized persecution for righteousness' sake, so severely condemned in the Scriptures? Why condemn such persecution at all, if wicked human governments have a moral right to inflict it? Besides, though the wicked relations of men are never regulated, but always condemned in the Scriptures, yet the behavior of innocent persons wrongfully subjected to them frequently is regulated, both by precept and example, see Ex. xxiii. 4; Prov. xx. 22, xxiv. 29; Matt. v. 39-44; Rom. xii. 17, 20, &c., and yet, so far from any license being granted in these passages to inflict the wrongs submitted to, we are assured in the same passages that God himself will avenge or punish them. Patient submission to oppression and other evil treatment is, according to the same and numerous corresponding passages, a moral duty which the oppressed and persecuted owe to God, and not to their oppressors, who persecute and oppress them. Were the doctrine otherwise, all who persecute and abuse their fellow-men "for righteousness sake" are, contrary to the plain teaching of the Scriptures, morally justified in such wickedness, so that even those who persecuted and put to death the Prophets, Apostles and martyrs, discharged none but their moral duty in so doing, and deserve praise instead of censure for such meritorious deeds!

# CHAPTER XVIII.

## PRO SLAVERY PERVERSIONS OF THE NEW TESTAMENT.
### (*Continued.*)

**Examination of Eph. vi. 5-9; Col. iii. 22-25, iv. 1; Titus ii. 9, 10; 1 Tim. vi. 1; 1 Pet. ii. 18-20.**

THE Greek words used in these passages for servants are *douloi*, plural of *doulos*, and *oiketai*, plural of *oiketes*, and for "masters," *kurioi*, plural of *kurios*, and *despotai*, plural of *despotes*--each couplet having apparently little or no distinction of meaning. Like our English word "servants," the two former never mean "slaves," whose technical Greek name as we have seen is *andrapoda*, unless the context and subject-matter show that fact--nor do the two latter ever mean "slaveholders," whose technical Greek word is *andrapodistai*, except where the same evidence proves that meaning. Thus the Apostles were not property or slaves in any sense, though each of them styled himself a "*servant*" (*doulos*) of Jesus Christ his "*master*" (*kurios)* who certainly was not a slaveholder in any sense, see Luke ii. 29; Acts ii. 18; Rom. i. 1; Phil. i. 1; Titus i. 1; James i. 1; 2 Pet. i. 1, &c., nor are those words ever used in the New Testament, in connection with any slavish regulations or directions. On the contrary, though the best directions are given in that volume for the good regulation of the *ordinary* FREE *relation of master and servant*, it cannot be possible they were intended to regulate the relation of *master* and *slave*, for if obeyed they would be sure to destroy the latter relation itself, contrary to the intent of all such regulations, which are always provided for their support and not their injury. Thus the simple direction given in Eph. vi. 9; Col. iv. 1; Philemon, 16th verse, would, if literally obeyed by all slaveholders, put a final and total end to their slaveholding rights and authority in a single day. Now we cannot honestly and innocently believe or suppose, that God would provide regulations for the intended support and benefit of any relation whatever, which He foreknew would if obeyed certainly overthrow and destroy it!! It must be highly wicked to imagine God capable of such folly. It is possible that the directions contained in Eph. vi. 5-8, were intended to apply to the cases of all servants alike, to that of slaves among the rest, because, according to the spirit of Matt. v. 39-44; Rom. xii. 17, 20, &c., it is the moral duty of slaves and other oppressed persons who cannot peaceably avoid their unhappy condition, patiently to submit to their hard fate, leaving the punishment of their oppressors to God, who will be sure to inflict it, because he has promised to do so.

But we should remember that these directions are accompanied by others to the masters, which if obeyed will be sure to terminate the relation, so that the whole directions taken together must have been intended to destroy slavery, because their joint effect is entirely antagonistical and hostile to the practice. The same passages also teach us, that whenever we address slaves on the subject of their moral duty in that condition, we should also address the masters on their moral duty in relation to their slaves, which according to the spirit of the passages, as well as that of the whole Scriptures, clearly is, to treat their slaves in all respects as freemen or free and voluntary servants, by allowing and respecting all their natural rights, which will of course terminate their enslavement. It is remarkable also that the duties of servants inculcated in the passages under consideration, are represented in them as due to God and not to man, from which circumstance I strongly suspect their directions were intended for slaves, more than for any other class of servants, especially as Asia

Minor, in which Ephesus was situated, abounded in slaves. Similar directions, and for similar reasons, are also given to all classes of servants and masters in Col. iii. 22, 25, iv. 1; Colosse being also a city of Asia Minor. Similar remarks are also in all respects applicable to the directions contained in Titus ii. 9, 10; 1 Pet. ii. 18-20, perfect obedience to which is sure instantly to destroy the practice of slavery, which effect was doubtless one of their principal objects. It is certainly very remarkable, that the principal, if not the only motive from which servants of all classes are required to act, is obedience to the will of God, and a desire that his name and religion might receive honor and credit, in which motive slaves as well as others ought to participate, though they owe no moral duty of slavish service on account of their masters or owners.

I have no doubt whatever that the "servants under the yoke," addressed in 1st Tim. vi. 1, 2, were real slaves, because the Roman ceremony of passing prisoners of war under the yoke, was used in token of their conversion into property or slaves, whence the figurative phrase "under the yoke" denoted their condition as such. As this was a pure heathen custom there could have been no intention to approbate it in this passage, though the latter is otherwise worthy of very critical attention.

We observe from the language of the passage, that these servants or slaves were directed to honor their heathen masters, not from any regard to the latter as deserving such respect, but from a much higher and more important motive, namely,--"that the name of God and his doctrine be not blasphemed," or in other words, that profane cursing, and swearing, and hatred of others, might be avoided, the same being the violation of the Third Commandment, most common among discontented slaves as well as among their idle and dissipated masters, especially when irritated. This passage was intended to regulate the behavior of servants, indeed, as the directions in Matt. v. 39-44; Rom. xii. 14, 19-21, &c., were that of oppressed persons in general, but it furnished no more moral justification or license to slavery, than these latter passages did to religious or other persecution for righteousness sake--a distinction readily understood in every other case except that of slavery. As additional evidence that the apostle had no design to regulate the practice of human slavery by these directions it is very remarkable that he gave no directions to masters at all in the passage, no doubt, for one very sufficient reason, that they held a sinful relation to their slaves which he had no moral right to countenance, which he could hardly fail to do by addressing them after such directions to their slaves. Thus, this and the preceding passages, which have been reviewed in this chapter, instead of being pro-slavery as so many contend, are directly the reverse, because they have the strongest anti-slavery tendency and effect.

From the phraseology "believing masters," which occurs in the passage last criticised, it has been sagaciously inferred in behalf of slavery, that Paul fellowshipped slaveholders, not only as Christian brethren, but as members of the Christian church, and thus morally countenanced the practice of human slavery. There is no doubt that some slaveholders, as well as other heathen, were converted by the reaching of this apostle, and remained such until they became convinced of the sinfulness of their slaveholding relations, but there is no evidence in this passage, or anywhere else, that Paul or the other apostles ever received them into church membership, before they discovered the sinfulness of slavery and renounced the practice of it. We see from his Epistles to the Corinthians,

Galatians, and others, that the great apostle to the gentiles had an immense deal of trouble with his new heathen converts, to wean them from the wicked heathen practices to which they have been so long customarily addicted, but we have no evidence that he admitted them to Christian church membership till they renounced those practices; while from the well known historical fact, that the early progress of Christianity destroyed the practice of human slavery, wherever the Christian doctrines were preached in their purity, the strong presumption is that he did not. There is no probability that the apostles fellowshipped persons as church members, who lived in the customary practice of sins and crimes condemned in their epistles, because we see from such passages as 2 Cor. vi. 14, 17, &c., that they excommunicated such persons and directed the other church members to shun their company. Why should they receive persons into church membership beforehand, whom they were sure, or almost sure, to excommunicate afterwards? We see from the principal passage, that there was great danger that the converted slaves would despise the converted owners, and why? Because the latter were a disgrace to the new religion they professed to have been converted to, and why? Because, although they had been converted to the true religion, they remained in the practice of a great sin utterly condemned by that religion, to the great disgrace of the latter, as well as injustice and injury to the slaves. Under such circumstances, nothing could be more necessary and proper than the directions of the apostles to these slaves, in order to prevent them as well as their masters disgracing the same holy religion. For these reasons I would just as soon believe that the same apostle, who, in 1 Tim. i. 9, 10, condemned slaveholders with the same moral severity he did the worst of other criminals, admitted the latter to church membership while living in the customary practice of their former sins, as that he admitted slaveholders to the same privilege while living in the practice of slavery. I would just as soon believe that this apostle continued a persecutor after his own conversion, as to believe in this pro-slavery pretence. It is certain that Paul had a great deal of difficulty, sorrow, and trouble, with his new converts from heathenism, on account of their idolatrous and other evil heathen habits, but he never, knowingly, admitted any of them to church fellowship and Christian communion until they had renounced those habits. The reception of new converts to church privileges is predicated in the New Testament on the entire change in their former evil sentiments and practices, testified to by their voluntary obedience to the commands of Christ, and manifestation of good works, as evidence of their genuine conversion, as is clear from such passages as Matt. iii. 8, 10, viii. 16, 20, xii, 33; John v. 29; Rom. ii. 6; 1 Cor. v. 1, 5, 9; 2 Cor. v. 10; Col. iii. 5-9; 1 John iii. 18, &c. The apostles being at all times under the immediate guidance and direction of the Holy Spirit of God, could never have knowingly violated the plain rule in their church organization, government, and discipline.

It is possible, though not at all probable, that the "believing masters" spoken of in this passage, had actually abandoned the practice of slavery. But whether they had or had not, the phrase is used in the sense of similar phraseology, so often occurring in common modern practice, of giving epithets to persons which have characterized their former lives, though radical changes have taken place in their characters and behavior. Thus the phrase "believing *Jew*," "converted *Infidel*," "reformed *drunkard*," &c., similar to the customary scriptural expressions, "the blind *see*," "the deaf *hear*," "the lame *walk*," &c., are nothing but nonsense if they be understood as literally true, just as the foregoing phrases must be on the same understanding, because nobody supposes that *converted infidels* and *reformed drunkards* retain the vicious practices they have been converted and reformed from. In like manner, it is unreasonable as well as unscriptural to suppose that "believing" or converted slaveholders in the apostles' time, continued in the practice of slavery after they discovered the sinfulness of it, though it is highly probable that many of them did before they made that important discovery.

# CHAPTER XIX.

## PRO-SLAVERY PERVERSIONS OF THE NEW TESTAMENT.
### (*Continued.*)

### Examination of the Epistle to Philemon.

GREAT reliance is placed by the advocates of human slavery on Paul's epistle to Philemon, as furnishing supposed evidence that the latter was a real slaveholder, and at the same time a member of the Christian church by the permission of the apostle himself. From these assumed premises they argue that the practice of human slavery cannot be a sin in itself, for if it were, the apostle would not have admitted Philemon to church membership. They also argue from the same premises, that the conduct of the Apostle in this case is a sufficient moral warrant for the forcible seizure and restoration of fugitive slaves. On account of the confidence with which these pro-slavery pretences are advanced, the whole of this short epistle deserves a very attentive and critical consideration.

A slight examination of the epistle assures us that Philemon was a member of the Christian church, but there is not a particle of evidence in it to prove that he was a slaveholder, but the reverse, as I shall soon show. Nor is there any evidence that Onesimus was a slave, but the reverse. The too common pro-slavery assumption that they respectively were such, is therefore a mere begging of the question; and that not only without, but against the evidence furnished by the same epistle.

I have already remarked, that as the Greek words "*doulos*" and "*oiketes*" literally mean "servants," we have no means of determining whether the persons designated in the New Testament by these words were free servants or slaves, except by the subject matter, by the context, and by the general description in the whole narrative. In this short epistle Onesimus is in the 16th verse called a "*doulos*" or man-servant simply, while in the postscript at the end of the epistle, which is supposed to have been the ancient superscription or direction to it, he is called an "*oiketes*," or house, or domestic servant, nothing more being indicated by either word to show the special nature of his servitude or service, to ascertain which, with any degree of reasonable probability, we are compelled to resort to the subject matter contained in the context, or rather to the whole epistle, which, so far as it goes, is clearly indicative, or descriptive, not of slavish, but of free service, and leaves no reasonable doubt of the fact that Onesimus was a free and voluntary servant of some kind. Some conjecture from the expression, "in the flesh," used in the same 16th verse, that Onesimus was a natural brother of Philemon, in which case there is no probability that the former was a slave, as the practice of enslaving such near relations was not as common among the ancient heathen as it now is among modem Christians. From the general description in the epistle there is no doubt but that he had quitted his master Philemon's service without leave, and had unjustly injured the latter, and done wrong thereby, which he could not have done if he were a slave, because it is next to impossible for a slave unjustly to injure his owner by quitting his service. All the real injustice is on the side of the master by retaining the slave in bondage, and none at all on the part of the slave in escaping from the same bondage in which he is held contrary to justice. Nor is it credible if Onesimus were a slave, that the Apostle should have blamed him for obeying the Levitical statute contained in Deut. xxiii. 15, 16, "Thou shalt not deliver unto his master the servant which has escaped from his master unto thee. He shall dwell with thee, even among you, in that place which he shall choose in one of thy gates, where it liketh him best, thou shalt not oppress him." See also 1 Cor. vii. 21, 23, where the same Apostle directed slaves to regain their liberty if they peaceably could. Ought we for a moment to believe that the Apostle who gave such directions, would have voluntarily assisted in restoring Onesimus to the same unhappy condition he had just escaped from; for this great Apostle not only acted consistently with his own teaching, but no man ever lived who knew better than he did both the natural and revealed injustice and criminality of slavery, or who did less to favor and support it? Besides, we see from the 18th and 19th verses of the epistle, that Onesimus could "owe" Philemon, which was impossible if he were a slave, but not only possible but very probable, if he were a free servant. There is not the slightest probability that the same Apostle, who, in 1 Tim. i. 9, 10, had characterized slavery as a crime equal to the worst kind of crimes, would have supposed Onesimus had done anything wrong in escaping from it, or would have advised him to return to it again. Fugitive slaves, when retaken and restored to their owners, were generally subjected to torture and other abuse in ancient as well as in modern times, a fate Paul would have been the last man in the world to assist in producing, especially on one of his own converts. As no man ever understood the Levitical law better than he did, and as he reverenced that law, he never would have violated the statute in Deut. xxiii. 15, 16. The whole course of conduct pursued by the Apostle in the case is entirely inconsistent and incredible, on the supposition that Onesimus was a slave, but entirely consistent and credible, because morally right and proper, on the contrary supposition that Onesimus was a free servant. What a wicked notion is that contended for by so many pro-slavery people, that the author of Romans xii. employed himself in enticing back and restoring fugitive slaves! Yet the conduct of the Apostle in this case is held up and quoted even by Christian Preachers, and professors of religion, as the moral model and justificatory example of all the slaveholders and slave-catchers in the world!

From the foregoing facts, taken in connection with the whole spirit and tenor of the epistle, there is not the slightest probability that Onesimus was a slave, or that Philemon was a slaveholder. The supposition that either were such is a libel on the Christian office and character of the Apostle Paul, and a wicked imputation on the special grace which gave him that office and character, see Acts xxii. 4, 5, 14; Gal. i. 13-16, &c.

From Paul's history and writings we have no more reason to believe that after his conversion he engaged in the practice of theft and other crimes than that he engaged in the fraudulent enticement or forcible seizure and restoration of fugitive slaves, the only effectual means ever employed to return such fugitives. Being as the Apostle to the Gentiles the greatest preacher of the only true religion in the world, he would never have countenanced any kind of heathen customs such as slavery, and all its incidents clearly are. For these reasons I do not know of a more absurd and wicked perversion of the Scriptures than that which represents the Apostles and their converts to a religion which is "first pure, then peaceable, gentle," &c. (James iii. 17), as engaged in the business of enticing, defrauding, seizing, and sending back innocent, heart-broken slaves, to their masters who were like our slaveholders.

# CHAPTER XX.

## CONCLUSION--REFLECTIONS.

THE pro-slavery scriptural perversions, which have now been exposed and refuted, are all that are worthy of special notice. They constitute the principal "refuge of lies" by which modern slavery has been morally justified among Christians; and now that they are effectually exploded, it is earnestly hoped and expected that the final overthrow of the system will be speedy and complete. These perversions have been the principal fortress of Christian slavery in modern times, the destruction of which will be a sure prelude to the fall of its idol. It will be comparatively easy to refute other pro-slavery pretences, because they all morally depend on the great perversions now destroyed. Well do the Scriptures represent such perversions, as among the greatest sins, not only on account of their wicked nature, but on account of their tremendous necessary tendency to destroy public and private happiness, which tendency was never more powerfully exemplified by anything than by the progress of modern Christian slavery. Chiefly on the credit and by the influence of these perversions, millions of human beings have been customarily robbed of their rights, their liberties, their happiness, and their lives, merely to gratify and pamper the wicked lusts of others, who have also been customarily corrupted and destroyed, by the same wicked gratifications, and thus more misery and destruction indicted on mankind by these, than by any other wicked causes. From such awful consequences, more perhaps than by anything else, we can easily discover and realize the dreadful enormity of the sin of scriptural perversion. As has been already remarked, these perversions were entirely of Catholic

origin, afterwards copied and adopted by all classes of Protestants, as sound theological doctrine-- which conduct, if it do not prove the Protestant churches to be the "Harlot" spoken of in Rev. xvii. 5, furnishes no proof that the Catholic church is the "Mother" mentioned in the same passage. The same perversions have produced a slaveholding priesthood and people, all over Christendom, and laid the foundation of slavery and oppression everywhere. They have produced a slaveholding Christianity, the propagation of which has been visibly followed by the displeasure of God, in every part of the world where the Christian religion now prevails--the same and similar perversions being also customarily employed, to justify the aristocratic oppression, the luxury, the lewdness, the dueling, the wars, and many other public vices so customarily prevalent in all Christian countries. Nor do these terrible effects stop here. It is in vain to preach this pro-slavery religion to the heathen, who will not receive it, as indeed they ought not-- for such religion not only morally justifies slavery itself, but also all other crimes necessary to support it, and must therefore, in the opinion of every intelligent heathen, be as false at least as his own religion; and operating thus to the special injury of the heathen by enslaving them, they will reject it with abhorrence and disdain. A religion so perverted, and falsified, and discredited, ought not to prevail, for all perversions of the true religion render it a false one, and a false religion is worse than none at all. Such fatal consequences show the extreme necessity of works like this, the design of which is to overthrow and destroy such destructive perversions.

Next to perversions, the most fatal mistake ever made in the science of the true theology, is the doctrine of neglecting and rejecting a part of the law of God in practice--for according to the precepts of that law, as revealed in the Pentateuch and ratified in the New Testament, it was designed to be universal, and to oblige every human being to obey the whole of it, see Gen. i. 26, 28, xii. 3, xxii. 18, xxvi. 3-5, xxviii. 14; Deut. xxvii. 26, xxviii. 1, 15; Jer. xi. 3, 4; Eze. xviii. 21; Matt. v. 17, 19; Rom. iii. 20, 21, 23; James ii. 10, &c., &c. These and numerous similar passages prove, that the promises made to Abraham extended to all mankind; that the *moral law* given to his posterity, was given to all; that it was to remain in force until the whole of it was fulfilled; that all mankind were bound to obey the whole and every part, of it, and that all had violated it and needed a Saviour. Now this law, as revealed in the Pentateuch, consists of three distinct parts:

- 1. The typical, figurative or ceremonial;
- 2. The religious or moral;
- 3. The practical or civil.

Of these three parts, the first only is fulfilled, by the advent and death of Christ, while none of the parts are repealed. The whole of this law is still in force, the political portion as well as the rest, and it is from want of conformity to it alone, that there is so much destruction and misery in the world. All the human laws in the world, which do not conform to this law, are morally null and void as wicked laws. But as no human code does thus conform, but has greatly deviated from God's law, all human codes are in many respects morally void, and it is a great sin thus to obey them. And so strict are the requirements of this great law, that the least deviation from it is held to be equivalent to a violation of the whole! What then are we to think of most human codes, as well as human actions?

To preserve obedience, and prevent disobedience to this great law, the true church is the great worldly agent appointed by God himself, see Matt. v. 13, 16, &c. From the various descriptions given of it in the Scriptures, we find, that by its own constitution it embodies the elements of all reformatory agencies, being of itself a Bible, Tract, Missionary, Temperance, Anti-Slavery, and Moral Reform Society, and is intended to perform all the functions of these agencies. But the very necessity of them, separate from the church, proves the melancholy fact, that the latter, instead of taking the lead, is following in the track of moral reform!! The pulpit is the place specially appointed by God, from which to attack slavery and other public vices, but it is not used for that purpose, because it has become corrupted by them. Woo to true moral reform, when the moral salt of the earth has lost its savor! Had the Christian church always done its duty in relation to public vices of every description, they would have been continually checked and destroyed, and the world kept in comparative peace and happiness. Much is said in the Scriptures about false prophets and false priests, who are represented and condemned as among the greatest of sinners, because their agency is more corrupt and corrupting than any other, see Neh. ix. 34; Jer. ii. 8, v. 31, xxxii. 32; Lam. iv. 13; Eze. xxii. 25-28; Matt. xxiv. 24; 2 Pet. ii. 1, &c. From the numerous passages of this kind occurring chiefly in the true Prophets, we find false priests uniformly described, as those who either neglect to teach the whole moral law, or else teach it falsely by perversions, and thus lead the people astray into customary sins, a description which ought to make most, if not all our Christian Preachers and teachers tremble--for which of them pretend to teach the whole moral law to their hearers? Some are unable for want of knowledge, but those who are able know the attempt would ruin their *popularity* at this corrupt period, and hence they either neglect or pervert a large part of the moral law to please their corrupt hearers. How then can they say with Paul (Acts xx. 26, 27), "I am pure from the blood of all men, for I have not shunned to declare unto you all the counsel of God."

If any portion of the Christian priesthood are now so ignorant, as honestly to believe in the perversions, which have here been exposed and refuted, they are "blind leaders of the blind," and ought to be silenced for incompetency as well as heresy. But on the other hand those of them who understand these perversions, but will not faithfully expose, and refute, and bear their official testimony against them, are even worse than the other class, being by exact description the "dumb" and "greedy dogs" alluded to in Isa. lvi. 10, 11, and the false priests and teachers mentioned in other passages, who for the sake of worldly popularity, ease, wealth, favor and patronage, wilfully neglect their plain official duty in this respect; and they ought for that reason also to be silenced. The religious services of these men must be worse than useless, because, if the very prayers and other religious services of the wicked are an abomination to the Lord (see Prov. xv. 8, xxviii. 9; Isa. i. 11-15, &c.), all such services and other religious exertions of those who believe in Scriptural slavery, or who pretend to, while they do not, and who justify human slavery on that ground, must be most heinously sinful, and only increase the moral guilt of those who practice them, without any just reason to expect the divine favor and blessing, but the reverse. In this terrible censure, I include Protestants equally with Catholics, because they are equally guilty in the propagation of these wicked perversions, and of the slaveholding practices consequent upon them. So far as I have been able to ascertain there is no essential difference in the amount of pro-slavery corruption, existing in each of these great divisions of the so called Christian church.

Human slavery, like most other public and customary sins, is entirely of heathen origin, having in modern times been originally adopted by modern Christians (in violation and defiance of their own religion, from the slaveholding customs of the heathen negroes in Africa), who afterwards justified and sustained it by the perversions which have been reviewed. Such slavery is also a state or condition of permament public and private war, as we know from the obvious fact, that it is at all times and under all circumstances, supported by public and private fraud, force and violence, and by no other means, as fully and as completely as any other form or mode of war is; and also from another fact equally striking, that it is equally destructive to the public prosperity and private happiness of every country that allows and pursues it, as any other kind of war is. The constant operation of all the evil passions engendered by it, between the enslavers and the enslaved, necessarily produces this effect, as has been fully exemplified in every slave country both in ancient and modern times. Hence both slaveholders and slaves are always discontented and unhappy. But besides this, it so interferes with all the free interests and policy of every country, in which it prevails, that none of these interests and policy can be harmonized with it and successfully pursued, so long as the curse is permitted to exist unchecked and uncontrolled. Thus, none of the great political measures, so much controverted in the United States, can ever be satisfactorily adjusted and settled, until slavery is entirely abolished and destroyed--the reason why human slavery possesses such immense political influence being because it is so highly political in its own nature, which is proved by the well known fact, that it has done, and is doing, more to diminish the public temporal prosperity of mankind, than any other single public institution in the world.

The belief is almost universally prevalent in the Christian world, because it is generally countenanced by the Christian clergy, that the Scriptures do not teach what is generally called "politics" or political action at all, and that Christians, as such, have nothing to do with such action--than which a greater heresy never existed, for the Bible is the strongest and best political book in the world. A book which utterly condemns all sins, political as well as others, must necessarily be a political book. The word "political" is not found in the Bible, to be sure, any more than the word "moral" is, because the first was not in the Hebrew and Latin, nor the last in the Greek language, but political action is just as strongly described in the Scriptures as moral action is--and they never separate those modes of action in description, as we customarily attempt to do, in our account of them, because they are really inseparable in their natures, as all their effects prove. This pamphlet, for instance, will be universally considered as of a moral nature, but nothing can be more highly political than its tendency, because that tendency is to destroy the greatest single political institution in the country. So is every other book of a political nature, the tendency of which is to affect or modify the public temporal interests of society. All public institutions which produce that effect are of the same nature, which the etymology of the words "politics," "policy," "political," &c., clearly proves. Another heresy, connected with this subject, also deserves exposure and reproof. Many persons, who acknowledge both the natural and revealed sinfulness of slavery, do yet contend, that no special exertions ought to be made against this public sin, because God will, in His own time and manner, deliver the oppressed slaves, as he has so often promised to do in the Scriptures. It is most true that God will eventually deliver the slaves, whether we repent of the sin of enslaving them or not; but the whole analogical teaching of the Scriptures, as well as the promises of God teach us, that He will do so by our own national destruction, unless we seasonably repent and reform from the sin of slavery by voluntary abolition. There are numerous cases of the Divine threats against the great sin of oppression recorded in the Scriptures, every one of which, with the exception of Nineveh, were carried into execution, and that exception was made only upon repentance and reformation--all the other cases being those of reprobation or a voluntary refusal to repent. All over the Scriptures reprobation and destruction are united together--the terrible threat in Prov. xxix. 1, being just as applicable to nations as to individuals. From the case of the Antediluvians recorded in Genesis to that of the mystical Mother of Harlots in the Revelation, not a single exception is made. The cases of Sodom and Gomorrah, of Pharaoh, of the wicked Jewish Kings, of Judea, Moab, Tyre, Egypt, Assyria, Babylon, &c. are all in point, as is the subsequent destruction of the Greeks, Carthaginians, Romans, &c., for the great sin of reprobation. From the analogy furnished by these terrible examples, we see clearly what our own national doom is to be, if we finally prove guilty of this terrible sin, in relation to our slavish oppressions; we being just as certain of national destruction from that cause, as the Antediluvians, Pharaoh, the Egyptians, the Jews, &c., were, unless we follow the example of Nineveh, and repent, and reform our lives, as well as our national character, which we have yet a little time and space to do. That the Lord, in his infinite goodness, may grant us the disposition to do it, is the prayer of the writer of these pages.